Pocket
HONG KONG

TOP SIGHTS · LOCAL LIFE · MADE EASY

Piera Chen, Emily Matchar

In This Book

QuickStart Guide

Your keys to understanding the city – we help you decide what to do and how to do it

Need to Know
Tips for a smooth trip

Neighbourhoods
What's where

Explore Hong Kong

The best things to see and do, neighbourhood by neighbourhood

Top Sights
Make the most of your visit

Local Life
The insider's city

The Best of Hong Kong

The city's highlights in handy lists to help you plan

Best Walks
See the city on foot

Hong Kong's Best...
The best experiences

Survival Guide

Tips and tricks for a seamless, hassle-free city experience

Getting Around
Travel like a local

Essential Information
Including where to stay

Our selection of the city's best places to eat, drink and experience:

⊙ **Sights**

⊗ **Eating**

⊙ **Drinking**

⊛ **Entertainment**

⊕ **Shopping**

These symbols give you the vital information for each listing:

☎ Telephone Numbers	👶 Family-Friendly
⊙ Opening Hours	🐾 Pet-Friendly
P Parking	🚌 Bus
⊘ Nonsmoking	⛴ Ferry
@ Internet Access	M Metro
🛜 Wi-Fi Access	S Subway
🥗 Vegetarian Selection	🚋 Tram
📖 English-Language Menu	🚆 Train

Find each listing quickly on maps for each neighbourhood:

Bar Hemingway

16 ⊙ Map p233, B2

Legend has it that Hemi self, wielding a machine orate this timber-pan ered bar during showpiece is a en by Papa ar town. Dress s.com; Hôtel Rit ⊙6.30pm-2a

Lonely Planet's Hong Kong

Lonely Planet Pocket Guides are designed to get you straight to the heart of the city.

Inside you'll find all the must-see sights, plus tips to make your visit to each one really memorable. We've split the city into easy-to-navigate neighbourhoods and provided clear maps so you'll find your way around with ease. Our expert authors have searched out the best of the city: walks, food, nightlife and shopping, to name a few. Because you want to explore, our 'Local Life' pages will take you to some of the most exciting areas to experience the real Hong Kong.

And of course you'll find all the practical tips you need for a smooth trip: itineraries for short visits, how to get around, and how much to tip the guy who serves you a drink at the end of a long day's exploration.

It's your guarantee of a really great experience.

Our Promise

You can trust our travel information because Lonely Planet authors visit the places we write about, each and every edition. We never accept freebies for positive coverage, so you can rely on us to tell it like it is.

QuickStart Guide   7

Explore Hong Kong   21

Worth a Trip:

QuickStart Guide

Welcome to Hong Kong

Hong Kong beckons and baffles, like the plot in one of its award-winning crime thrillers. Behind the city's futuristic facade hide smoky temples, surf-beaten beaches and sprawling, cattle-graced country parks. Hong Kong quickens the blood, yet reassures with the rule of law, an unbeatable transport system and the world's very best dim sum.

Downtown Hong Kong at sunset
COLOURSINMYLIFE/SHUTTERSTOCK ©

Hong Kong
Top Sights

Star Ferry (p24)

At only HK$2.50, the 15-minute ride on the legendary Star Ferry, with its views of the urban coastline and the shimmering waters of Victoria Harbour, must be one of the world's best-value cruises.

Tsim Sha Tsui East Promenade (p96)

This wave-kissed walkway is *the* place for viewing Hong Kong's best-known imagery: gleaming geometric skyscrapers lined up between dark emerald hills and a sapphire harbour crisscrossed by ships.

Victoria Peak (p42)

Take Hong Kong's oldest thrill ride, the Peak Tram, for an almost straight-up ascent to the summit and the Peak Tower, where you're greeted by postcard-perfect views of the city and the harbour.

HSBC Building (p26)

Designed by star architect Norman Foster, this impressive feat of high-tech modernism in glass and steel is one of Hong Kong's most iconic buildings and is home to the HSBC headquarters.

Man Mo Temple (p28)

This Taoist temple mesmerises with a bitter-sweet history and smoky air infused by incense coils suspended from the ceiling like inverted mushrooms in a strange garden.

Ruins of the Church of St Paul (p130)

Macau's most famous landmark is, rightfully, this gorgeous facade decorated with intricate carvings and detailed engravings; it was once part of a 17th-century Jesuit church.

Hong Kong Park (p64)

One of the most unusual parks in the world, emphasising creations such as its fountain plaza, conservatory, artificial ponds and waterfalls, children's playground and taichi garden.

Temple Street Night Market (p114)

Stalls sell a myriad of booty, from alarm clocks to bejeweled daggers, while fortune tellers summon from dimly lit tents.

Happy Valley Racecourse (p62)

Even if you don't bet, attending an electrifying Wednesday evening meeting at this urban racecourse is one of the most exhilarating things to do in Hong Kong.

TIM MARTIN/GETTY IMAGES ©

EVGENIA BOLYUKH/SHUTTERSTOCK ©

Sik Sik Yuen Wong Tai Sin Temple (p124)

A bustling temple dedicated to a healer who could turn sheep into stones. Watch Taoist rituals being performed or have your fortune told here.

Tian Tan Buddha (p126)

'Big Buddha' is the world's largest seated outdoor bronze Buddha. He occupies a hilltop spot on beautiful Lantau Island, but you can also see him as you fly into Hong Kong on a clear day.

Hong Kong
Local Life

Insider tips to help you find the real city

Alongside the top sights, you can experience Hong Kong like a local by exploring the coolest hang-outs, the pet beaches, the favourite mountain trails and those little indulgences that make up a Hong Konger's perfect day.

LKF & Soho Bar Crawl (p49)

▶ Swinging '60s
▶ Meet local activists

Drinking spots frequented by Hong Kong's revered revelers: sometimes the draw is the crazy crowd, sometimes it's the mural by a local artist, but often it is because the place could only exist in Hong Kong.

Wan Chai Breather (p66)

▶ Gadget Shopping
▶ Rent-a-Curse Grannies

Wan Chai's older quarter is filled with opportunities for hard-working Hong Kongers to regain peace of mind, from great gadget shopping and delicious food to folk sorcery that settles disputes.

Beach-Hopping on Island South (p84)

▶ Stanley Market
▶ Middle & South Bay

With beaches running from west to east, the southern coast of Hong Kong Island offers a seaside bazaar, a scenic promenade, plenty of windsurfing and kayaking opportunities and, of course, fine sands and clean water.

Exploring Taipa & Coloane Islands (p132)

▶ Taipa Village
▶ Coloane's Stilt Houses

Stilt houses, roadside temples, chapels squeezed into alleys, and museums by the waterfront – all within a ten-step radius of tempting Macanese food – dot the landscape of Macau's islands of Taipa and Coloane.

Stanley Market (p85),

Chapel of St Francis Xavier, Coloane Village (p133)

Other great places to experience the city like a local:

LGBT Hong Kong (p56)

Wan Chai's Markets (p74)

Street Music Concert Series (p77)

Sampan Tours (p88)

Dairy Farm Tour (p90)

Multicultural Kowloon (p105)

Poor Man's Peninsula (p110)

Getting Inked in Hong Kong (p118)

Hong Kong
Day Planner

Day One

☀ Catch the legendary Peak Tram up to **Victoria Peak** (p42) for stunning views of the city. Then descend and walk to Sheung Wan, checking out the dried seafood shops, the antique stores, and the trendy cafes along the way. Stop at **Man Mo Temple** (p28), one of Hong Kong's most important houses of worship, for a taste of the city's unique Chinese and colonial heritage. Then explore the old coffin shop and the hipster boutiques in the burgeoning community on **Tai Ping Shan Street** (p144).

☀ Take the **Star Ferry** (p176) to Kowloon. Enjoy the iconic views of the harbour along **Tsim Sha Tsui East Promenade** (p96) and savour your stroll to the resourceful **Museum of History** (p99) where you'll get some context to your day's impressions.

☾ Take the tram to **Soho** for drinks, dancing and live music. Swing by **Senses 99** (p56) to see if there's a gig on, or to show off your drumming or guitar skills if there's none.

Day Two

☀ Embrace (man-made) nature at lovely **Hong Kong Park** (p64), not forgetting to check out the **Museum of Tea Ware** (p65), then head over to Queen's Rd East to explore the sights and streets of this older part of **Wan Chai** (p146). Then take the tram to **Causeway Bay** for some shopping. Don't miss the speciality shops of **Caroline Haven** (p73).

☀ Take a peek inside **Chungking Mansions** (p110). Then relax and people-watch at the **Tsim Sha Tsui East Promenade** (p96) if construction has finished, or the **Middle Road Children's Playground** (p102) if you have a child, before taking afternoon tea in style at the **Peninsula** (p100). If the queue for a table is too long, the **InterContinental Lobby Lounge** (p109) serves tea too, with excellent harbour views. After that bus it north to **Yau Ma Tei**, where you can check out **Tin Hau Temple** (p118), the **Jade Market** (p122) and traditional shops along **Shanghai Street**.

☾ Have your fortune told and catch some Cantonese opera at **Temple Street Night Market** (p114). Then it's on to atmospheric **Butler** (p108) for a crafted Japanese cocktail or two.

Short on time?
We've arranged Hong Kong's must-sees into these day-by-day itineraries to make sure you see the very best of the city in the time you have available.

Day Three

Take the bus to **Aberdeen** for a cruise on the lovely Aberdeen Harbour. Follow with shopping (for bargain designer furniture and brand-name clothing) at **Horizon Plaza** (p93) on the island of Ap Lei Chau. Coffee and cakes are available at several of the furniture shops here. If it's a Saturday, take a boozy tour of Hong Kong's own brewery, **Young Master Ale** (p88).

After lunch, take the MTR to Wong Tai Sin for a lingering look at the **Sik Sik Yuen Wong Tai Sin Temple** (p124). Enjoy the ornate roofs and pillars, the zigzag bridge and the incense-infused atmosphere of this Taoist temple. Then divine your future by shaking a canister (until a fortune stick slides out). Readers will interpret your fortune for you.

Head to **Aqua** (p108) in Tsim Sha Tsui for a glamorous night out with sweeping views. Alternatively see what the local kids are up to at **Amuse** (p108). After a few drinks, late-night Korean fried chicken at **Chicken** (p105) **HOF & Soju Korean** (p105) may be music to your ears.

Day Four

Hop on an early boat to Macau. When you arrive, take a bus or a cab to the legendary **Lung Wah Teahouse.** (p140) Have dim sum for breakfast. Buy some tea leaves before you go and explore the bustling **Red Market** (p139) next door. Have a leisurely stroll to the cultural parts of **northern Macau Peninsula** (p136) to work off your breakfast. Check out the designer shops and the cobbled streets of the atmospheric **St Lazarus Church District** (p137), and buy a few souvenirs.

Head to the historic **Leal Senado** (p136) building, opposite Largo do Senado. Walk along Rua Central through much of the Unesco-listed **Historic Centre of Macau**, including the **ruins of the Church of St Paul** (p130). Nibble on Portuguese egg tarts and almond cookies as you do so. Then head to lovely **Taipa Village** (p132) for a look.

Check out the brand new **Studio City** (p141) casino complex. Try your hand at the tables or just have a drink at the bar. Then head back to Macau Peninsula to catch the ferry back to Hong Kong.

Need to Know

For more information, see Survival Guide (p173)

Currency
Hong Kong dollar (HK$) for Hong Kong, pataca (MOP$) for Macau.

Language
Cantonese, English and Mandarin. Also Portuguese for Macau.

Visas
Not required for visitors from the US, Australia, New Zealand, Canada, the EU, Israel and South Africa for stays of up to 30 days.

Money
ATMs widely available. Credit cards accepted in most hotels and restaurants; some budget places only take cash.

Mobile Phones
Any GSM-compatible phone can be used here. Set your phone to roaming, or buy a local SIM card if you need to make lots of calls. To make International Direct Dial (IDD) calls, buy a phonecard from PCCW stores or convenience stores.

Time
Hong Kong Time (GMT/UTC plus eight hours). Hong Kong does not have daylight-saving time.

Tipping
Taxi drivers only expect you to round up to the nearest dollar. Many restaurants add a 10% service charge to the bill.

① Before You Go

Your Daily Budget

Budget less than HK$800
▶ Guesthouse HK$180–450
▶ Meal at *cha chaan tang* (tea house) HK$60–150
▶ Bus, tram, ferry ride HK$2.50–15

Midrange HK$800–1800
▶ Double room at budget hotel HK$550–1100
▶ Chinese dinner with three dishes HK$350
▶ Drinks and live music HK$300

Top end more than HK$1800
▶ Double room in four-star or boutique hotel HK$2000
▶ Dinner at top Chinese restaurant from HK$800

Useful Websites

▶ **Lonely Planet** (www.lonelyplanet.com/hong-kong, www.lonelyplanet.com/china/macau) Destination info, hotel bookings etc.
▶ **Discover Hong Kong** (www.discoverhong-kong.com) Official Tourism Board website.
▶ **Hong Kong Observatory** (www.hko.gov.hk) Weather information.

Advance Planning

Two months before Check dates of festivals; book accommodation, tickets for major shows, and table at a top restaurant.

One month before Book tickets for fringe festivals and table at a popular restaurant.

Two weeks before Book harbour cruises; sign up for email alerts from events.

One week before Check the weather forecast.

2 Arriving in Hong Kong

Fly into Hong Kong International Airport (HKIA; www.hongkongairport.com), or cross the border at Lo Wu or Lok Ma Chau from Shenzhen on mainland China by bus or train (www.mtr.com.hk).

At Hong Kong International Airport, Customer Services Centres (arrivals hall 7am-11pm, departures hall 5am-1am) provide maps; money-exchange and banking counters; ATMs; and phones. Counters at the arrivals hall help with accommodation or car hire. Luggage storage facility (5.30am-1.30am) on Level 3 of Terminal 2.

✈ From Hong Kong International Airport

Destination	Best Transport
Central	Airport Express; Air Bus A11
Sheung Wan, Wan Chai, Causeway Bay	Airport Express then taxi; Air Bus A11
Aberdeen and the South	Air Bus A10
Tsim Sha Tsui, Yau Ma Tei, Mong Kok	Airport Express then taxi; Air Bus A21

🚃 From Lo Wu & Lok Ma Chau border gates

Destination	Best Transport
Admiralty, Central, Tsim Sha Tsui	MTR East Line to Kwun Tong Line to Tsuen Wan Line
Wan Chai, Causeway Bay	Change at Admiralty to Island Line
Yau Ma Tei, Mong Kok	MTR East Line to Kwun Tong Line
Sheung Wan and Sai Ying Pun	MTR to Sheung Wan, change to the West Island Line

3 Getting Around

Hong Kong's efficient Mass Transit Railway (MTR) system and comprehensive bus network will take you almost anywhere you need to go. A prepaid Octopus card can be used on most forms of public transport. MTR stations also sell one-day passes (adult/child HK$65/45) for unlimited rides on the MTR.

🚕 Taxi

Cheap compared to Europe and North America. Most are red; green ones operate in parts of the New Territories; blue ones on Lantau Island. All run on meter.

🚇 MTR

Hong Kong's Mass Transit Railway (MTR) system covers most of the city and is the easiest way to get around. Most lines run from 6am to after midnight.

🚌 Bus

Relatively fast, buses are an indispensable form of transport to places not reachable by the MTR or after midnight.

🚋 Tram

Offers slow but scenic rides along the northern strip of Hong Kong Island, from 6am to midnight.

⛴ Ferry

The Star Ferry connects Hong Kong Island and Kowloon Peninsula via Victoria Harbour. Ferry fleets also run between Central and the outlying islands.

Hong Kong
Neighbourhoods

Hong Kong Island: Lan Kwai Fong & Soho (p44)
Art galleries, stylish bars and local life as it has been for decades grace the streets of Hong Kong's partying epicentre.

Hong Kong Island: Central & Sheung Wan (p22)
Central: high finance meets haute couture; Sheung Wan: temples, antiques, dried seafood and funeral products.

👁 Top Sights

Star Ferry

HSBC Building

Man Mo Temple

Trip to Macau (p128)

👁 Top Sights

Ruins of the Church of St Paul

Temple Street Night Market

Star Ferry

Man Mo Temple

HSBC Building

Victoria Peak

Hong Kong Park

Hong Kong Island: Admiralty, Wan Chai & Causeway Bay (p60)
Admiralty has a restored explosives magazine; Wan Chai buzzes with markets, nightlife and multilingual kitchens; in Causeway Bay, shoppers shop.

👁 Top Sights

Happy Valley Racecourse

Hong Kong Park

Kowloon: Yau Ma Tei & Mong Kok (p112)

A famous night market and a leafy temple define Yau Ma Tei; Mong Kok offers sardine-packed commercialism.

◉ Top Sights

Temple Street Night Market

Worth a Trip

◉ Top Sights

Victoria Peak (p42)

Sik Sik Yuen Wong Tai Sin Temple (p124)

Tian Tan Buddha (p126)

Tsim Sha Tsui East Promenade

Kowloon: Tsim Sha Tsui (p94)

Sophisticated, with great museums, iconic views, colonial gems and all of Central's superlatives on a more human scale.

◉ Top Sights

Tsim Sha Tsui East Promenade

Happy Valley Racecourse
◉

Hong Kong Island: Aberdeen & the South (p82)

Attractive beaches, a seafront bazaar, sampan cruises in a typhoon shelter, one of Asia's best theme parks and awesome seafood.

Explore
Hong Kong

Worth a Trip

Mong Kok (p112)
LITTLEWORMY/SHUTTERSTOCK ©

Explore

Hong Kong Island: Central & Sheung Wan

The business heart of Hong Kong, sharp-suited Central is a heady mix of brand-name boutiques, gourmet restaurants, corporate cathedrals, and historic buildings (including a real cathedral). Arguably even more rewarding to explore, Sheung Wan carries the echo of 'Old Hong Kong', with its traditional shops, delicious temples and steep 'ladder streets', composed entirely of stairs.

The Sights in a Day

If it's a weekday, avoid taking the MTR during rush hour (7.30am to 9am). Visit **Man Mo Temple** (p28) and the Tai Ping Shan St temples; watch elders come to light their morning incense. Explore the neighbourhood. Beat the noon-to-2pm crowds by dining early at City Hall Maxim's Palace p35 before diving into the **Maritime Museum** (p32).

Admire classical Chinese furniture at **Liangyi Museum** (p33) if you've made an appointment. Then browse trinkets on **Cat Street** (p34). Over the next two hours, check out Central's modern and colonial-era architecture in the afternoon light, before indulging in retail therapy at a shopping mall.

Have dinner at **The Boss** (p36), followed by drinks at **Quinary** (p55).

Top Sights

Star Ferry (p24)

HSBC Building (p26)

Man Mo Temple (p28)

Best of Hong Kong

Eating

City Hall Maxim's Palace (p35)

Lung King Heen (p37)

The Boss (p36)

Views

Bank of China Tower (p32)

Two IFC (p35)

Getting There

Ⓜ **Metro** Central station (Island and Tsuen Wan lines); Hong Kong station (Airport Express); Sheung Wan station (Island line).

🚌 **Bus** Island buses stop at Central bus terminus (Exchange Sq); bus 26 links Central with Sheung Wan.

🚃 **Tram** Along Des Voeux Rd Central and Des Voeux Rd West.

⚓ **Star Ferry** From Tsim Sha Tsui to Central Pier 7.

Top Sights
Star Ferry

You can't say you've 'done' Hong Kong until you've taken a ride on a Star Ferry, that legendary fleet of electric-diesel vessels with names such as *Morning Star* and *Twinkling Star*. At any time of the day the ride, with its riveting views of skyscrapers and mountains, must be one of the world's best-value cruises. At the end of the 10-minute journey, watch as a hemp rope is cast and caught with a billhook, the way it was done in 1888 when the first boat docked.

天星小輪

◉ Map p30, G1

☎ 852 2367 7065

www.starferry.com.hk

adult HK$2.50-3.40, child HK$1.50-2.10

🕑 every 6-12 min, 6.30am-11.30pm

Ⓜ Hong Kong, exit A2

PASSENGERS SHOULD TAKE CARE WHEN CROSSING THE GANGWAY. 小心通跳板

Star Ferry's Stars

The Star Ferry was founded in 1888 by Dorabjee Nowrojee, a Parsee from Bombay. At the time most locals were crossing the harbour on sampans. Nowrojee bought a steamboat for his private use, and this eventually became the first Star Ferry. Parsees believe in the Persian religion of Zoroastrianism, and the five-pointed star on the logo is in fact an ancient Zoroastrian symbol.

Kowloon Concourse

In 1910 the Kowloon–Canton Railway was built near the Kowloon concourse, linking Hong Kong with the mainland. On Christmas Day 1941 the colonial governor took the ferry to Tsim Sha Tsui, where he surrendered to the Japanese at the Peninsula. You can still see the **Clock Tower** (前九廣鐵路鐘樓; Tsim Sha Tsui Star Ferry Concourse, Tsim Sha Tsui; 🚢 Star Ferry, Ⓜ East Tsim Sha Tsui, exit J) of the original train station here.

In 1966 thousands gathered at the Tsim Sha Tsui pier to protest a proposed 5c fare increase. It evolved into a riot on Nathan Rd, which is now seen as the trailblazer of local social protests leading to colonial reforms.

The Piers

The pier is an uninspiring Edwardian replica that replaced the old Edinburgh Pl pier, which had a clock tower. The old pier was demolished despite vehement opposition from Hong Kongers. The Kowloon pier remains untouched.

☑ **Top Tips**

▶ Snag a seat on the right side of the ferry when headed to Tsim Sha Tsui for the best views.

▶ The upper deck is well worth the extra few cents, for better views and fewer fumes.

▶ If you get on the ferry from Tsim Sha Tsui to Hong Kong just after 8pm you'll get front row seats to the nightly Symphony of Lights light show.

✗ **Take a Break**

▶ Fill up on dim sum at Tim Ho Wan (p38) before or after your (eight-minute) voyage.

Top Sights
HSBC Building

The stunning HSBC headquarters, designed by British architect Norman Foster in 1985, is a masterpiece of precision and innovation. And so it should be. On completion it was the world's most expensive building (costing US$1 billion). The 52-storey building reflects the architect's wish to create areas of public and private space, and to break the mould of bank architecture. A lighting scheme fitted later enables the building to maintain its splendour at night.

滙豐銀行總行大廈

◉ Map p31, F4

www.hsbc.com.hk

1 Queen's Rd, Central

admission free

⏱escalator 9am-4.30pm Mon-Fri, 9am-12.30pm Sat

Ⓜ Central, exit K

Stephen & Stitt

The two bronze lions guarding the main entrance were designed for the bank's previous headquarters in 1935. The lions are known as Stephen – the one roaring – and Stitt, after two bank employees at the time. The Japanese used the lions as target practice during the occupation; you can still see the shrapnel scars. Rub their mighty paws for luck.

Feng Shui

The building is full of examples of good feng shui (Chinese geomancy). There's no structure blocking its view of Victoria Harbour because water is associated with prosperity. The escalators are believed to symbolise the whiskers of a dragon sucking wealth into its belly. They're built at an angle to the entrance, supposedly to disorient evil spirits which can only travel in a straight line.

Lighting

The 52-storey glass-and-aluminium building was installed with around 700 lighting units, including colour-changing fluorescent lights,18 years after it was built. The project, costing $5.5 million, has ensured the building continues to dazzle as much at night as it does in broad daylight.

Atrium

The atrium, located on the 3rd floor, has greenery cascading from the different floors and is flooded with natural light. There's no prettier setting in which to get your money changed.

☑ Top Tips

▶ The cranes on the roof were allegedly placed there to combat the bad feng shui from the knife-like Bank of China building nearby.

▶ Find out whether there's any political controversy brewing in town by looking for protesters in the bank's public atrium, a popular spot for demonstrations.

✖ Take a Break

▶ For drinks with million-dollar views of the HSBC Building, plant yourself on the terrace of Sevva (p38), just across the street

Top Sights
Man Mo Temple

One of Hong Kong's oldest temples and a declared monument, atmospheric Man Mo Temple is dedicated to the god of literature (Man), who's always holding a writing brush, and the god of war (Mo), who wields a sword. Built by wealthy Chinese merchants in 1847 during the Qing dynasty, it was, besides a place of worship, a court of arbitration for local disputes in the 19th century when trust was thin between the local Chinese and the colonialists. Oaths taken at this Taoist temple (accompanied by the ritual beheading of a rooster) were accepted by the colonial government.

文武廟

◉ Map p30, C3

☎ 852 2540 0350

124-126 Hollywood Rd, Sheung Wan

admission free

🕗 8am-6pm

🚌 26

Incense coils in Man Mo Temple

Outside the Main Entrance

Here are four gilt plaques on poles that used to be carried during processions. Two describe the gods being worshipped, one requests silence and a show of respect, and the last warns menstruating women to keep out of the main hall as the blood is believed to put them in a state of ritual defilement.

Main Hall

In the main hall are two gold-plated sedan chairs that were used to carry statues of the deities during festivals. Suspended from the ceiling, like strange fungi in an upside-down garden, are rows of large earth-coloured incense coils.

Lit Shing Kung

Off to the side of the main hall is 'saints' palace', built around the same time as the temple. It's a place of worship for other Buddhist and Taoist deities, including the goddess of mercy and Tai Sui, the 60 heavenly generals who each represent a particular year in the 60-year cycle.

Kung Sor

The name of this hall means 'public meeting place'. The building was used to serve as a court of justice to settle disputes in the Chinese community before the introduction of the modern judicial system. A couplet at the entrance urges those entering to leave their selfish interests and prejudices outside.

☑ Top Tips

▶ There are fortune-telling sticks to the right of the main altar – slowly shake a stick out of the jar, then read the corresponding fortune in the (English) book.

▶ As with all Chinese temples, don't step directly on the door's high threshold, but over it – the threshold is meant to keep bad spirits away.

....

✖ Take a Break

▶ Relax with a cuppa at **Teakha** (茶家; ☎ 852 2858 9185; http://teakha.com; Shop B, 18 Tai Ping Shan St, Sheung Wan; ⏰ 11am-7pm Tue-Sun; 🛜; 🚌 26).

A
B
C
D

Connaught Rd West

Hong Kong-Macau
Ferry Terminal

1

Des Voeux Rd West

Wilmer St

Sutherland St

Ko Shing St

Bonham Strand West

New Market St

Wing Lok St

Wan Kei Ho
International
Martial Arts
Association

Connaught Rd Central

Shun Tak
Centre

Morrison St

●8

Sheung
Wan

23● Queen's Rd West

Hospital Rd

Hollywood Rd

Hollywood
Road
Park

**SHEUNG
WAN**

●24

Bonham Strand East

Hiller St

Man Wa La

Wing Lok St

2

New St

Po Yan St

Pak Sing
Ancestral Hall

●4

13●

✕12

Wa La

Sai

Tung St

Tai Ping Shan St

Tank La

Liangyi
Museum

5●●

●7

Cat
Street

Cleverly St

25
●

Jervois St

Gough St

Wing

20
✕

Pound La

Po Hing Fong

21

Ladder St

Bridges St

Wing Lee St

Shing St

Wong

**Man Mo
Temple**

Aberdeen St

Staunton St

Hollywood Rd

Gage St

Peel St

26
●

Old Bailey

3

Breezy Path

Bonham Rd

Park Rd

Conduit Rd

Seymour Rd

Castle Rd

Robinson Rd

SOHO

Peel St

Shelley St

Elgin St

Leung Fai Tce

Chancer

Caine Rd

4

Pok Fu Lam
Country
Park

Mosque St

Mosque Jct

**THE MID-
LEVELS**

5

For reviews see

●	Top Sights	p24
●	Sights	p32
✕	Eating	p35
●	Drinking	p38
●	Shopping	p39

THE PEAK

Ⓝ 0 ———————— 400 m
0 ———————— 0.25 miles

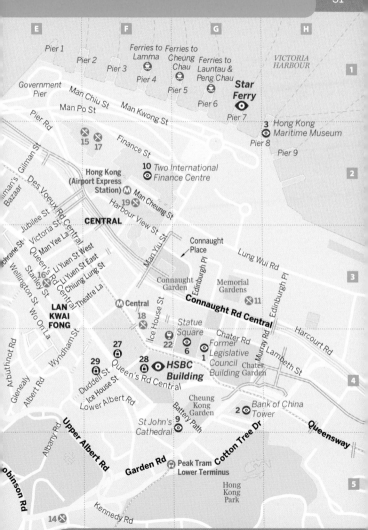

E   **F**   **G**   **H**

Pier 1

Pier 2

Ferries to Lamma

Ferries to Cheung Chau

Ferries to Lautau & Peng Chau

VICTORIA HARBOUR

Pier 3

Pier 4

Government Pier

Man Chiu St

Man Po St

Man Kwong St

Pier 5

Pier 6

Star Ferry

Pier 7

Pier Rd

15

17

Finance St

3 Hong Kong Maritime Museum

Pier 8

Pier 9

Tinman's Gilman St

Des Voeux Rd Central

10 Two International Finance Centre

Hong Kong (Airport Express Station)

Man Cheung St

Tinman's Bazaar

Jubilee St

Victoria St

Cochrane St

Queen's Rd Central

Man Yee Lane

Li Yuen St West

Li Yuen St East

Cleverly St

Chiuang Lung St

Theatre La

Stanley St

Wellington St

Wo On La

19

CENTRAL

Harbour View St

Man Yiu St

Connaught Place

Lung Wui Rd

Connaught Garden

Edinburgh Pl

Memorial Gardens

Edinburgh Pl

16

LAN KWAI FONG

Wyndham St

Theatre La

Central

18

Ice House St

Connaught Rd Central

11

Statue Square

22

Chater Rd

6

Former Legislative Council Building

Murray Rd

Lambeth St

Harcourt Rd

Chater Garden

Arbuthnot Rd

Glenealy

Albert Rd

27

29

Duddell St

28

Ice House St

Queen's Rd Central

HSBC Building

Lower Albert Rd

Cheung Kong Garden

2

Bank of China Tower

Queensway

Albany Rd

Robinson Rd

Upper Albert Rd

St John's Cathedral

9

Battery Path

Garden Rd

Peak Tram Lower Terminus

Cotton Tree Dr

Hong Kong Park

14

Kennedy Rd

1

2

3

4

5

Sights

Former Legislative Council Building
HISTORIC BUILDING

1 ◎ Map p30, G4

The colonnaded and domed building (c 1912) was built of granite quarried on Stonecutters' Island, and served as the seat of the Legislative Council from 1985 to 2012. During WWII it was a headquarters of the Gendarmerie, the Japanese version of the Gestapo, and many people were executed here. Standing atop the pediment is a blindfolded statue of Themis, the Greek goddess of justice and natural law. (前立法會大樓; 8 Jackson Rd, Central; Ⓜ Central, exit G)

Bank of China Tower
NOTABLE BUILDING

2 ◎ Map p30, G4

The awesome 70-storey Bank of China Tower, designed by IM Pei, rises from the ground like a cube, and is then successively reduced, quarter by quarter, until the south-facing side is left to rise on its own. Some geomancers believe the four prisms are negative symbols; being the opposite of circles, these triangles contradict what circles suggest – money, union and perfection. (中銀大廈, BOC Tower; 1 Garden Rd, Central; Ⓜ Central, exit K)

Hong Kong Maritime Museum
MUSEUM

3 ◎ Map p30, H2

Relocation and expansion have turned this into one of the city's strongest museums, with 15 well-curated galleries detailing over 2000 years of Chinese maritime history and the development of the Port of Hong Kong. Exhibits include ceramics from China's ancient sea trade, shipwreck treasures and old nautical instruments. A painted scroll depicting piracy in China in the early 19th century is one of Hong Kong's most important historical artefacts, and, like the rest of the museum, a real eye-opener. (香港海事博物館; ☎852 3713 2500; www.hkmaritimemuseum.org; Central Ferry Pier 8, Central; adult/child & senior HK$30/15; ◷9.30am-5.30pm Mon-Fri, 10am-7pm Sat & Sun; ♿; Ⓜ Hong Kong, exit A2)

Pak Sing Ancestral Hall
TEMPLE

4 ◎ Map p30, B2

In the 19th century, many Chinese who left home in search of better horizons died overseas. As it was the wish of traditional Chinese to be buried in their home towns, this temple was built in 1856 to store corpses awaiting burial in China, and to serve as a public ancestral hall for those who could not afford the expense of bone repatriation. Families of the latter have erected 3000 memorial tablets for their ancestors in a room behind the altar. (廣福祠; Kwong Fuk Ancestral Hall; 42 Tai Ping Shan St, Sheung Wan; ◷8am-6pm; ☒26)

Hong Kong Maritime Museum

Liangyi Museum
MUSEUM

5 Map p30, C2

This private three-floor museum houses two exquisite collections – antique Chinese furniture from the Ming and Qing dynasties, and Chinese-inspired European vanities from the 19th and 20th century. The former is one of the world's best. The 400 pieces of precious *huanghuali* and zitan furniture are shown in rotating exhibitions that change every six months. The only way to visit is by contacting the museum at least a day in advance to join a small tour. (兩依博物館; ☎852 2806 8280; www. liangyimuseum.com; 181-199 Hollywood Rd, Soho; admission HK$200; ⊙10am-6pm Tue-Sat; ⓂCentral, exit D2)

Statue Square
SQUARE

6 Map p30, G4

This leisurely square used to house effigies of British royalty. Now it pays tribute to a single sovereign – the founder of HSBC. In the northern area (reached via an underpass) is the **Cenotaph** (和平紀念碑; Chater Rd; ⓂCentral, exit A), built in 1923 as a memorial to Hong Kong residents killed during the two world wars. On the south side of Chater Rd, Statue Sq has a pleasant collection of fountains and seating areas, with tiling that's strangely reminiscent of a 1980s municipal washroom. (皇后像廣場; Edinburgh Pl, Central; ⓂCentral, exit K)

Understand
Chug Chug Ding A Ling

Nicknamed 'ding dings' by locals, trams have been sedately chugging back and forth between the Eastern and Western districts of the island since 1904. More than a century on, the world's largest fleet of double-decker tramcars – and Hong Kong's lowest-carbon transport option – continues to negotiate pathways through the city's heavy traffic.

For a flat fare (dropped in a box as you disembark, or use an Octopus card) you can rattle along as far as you like over 16km of track along the northern coast of Hong Kong Island.

Board a 'ding ding' and watch the city unfold like a carousel of images. Try to get a seat at the front window on the upper deck for the best view. Observing the districts east of Causeway Bay from a moving tram imparts a cinematic quality that seeing these primarily residential districts on foot may not. The bonus is that you can hop off whenever you feel like.

Hong Kong Tramways (☏852 2548 7102; www.hktramways.com; fares HK$2.30; ⊙6am-midnight) also offers an hour-long TramOramic tour that lets you experience the city on an open-top, faux-vintage tram.

Cat Street AREA

7 ◉ Map p30, C2

Just north of (and parallel to) Hollywood Rd is Upper Lascar Row, aka 'Cat Street', a pedestrian-only lane lined with antique and curio shops and stalls selling found objects, cheap jewellery and newly minted ancient coins. It's a fun place to trawl through for a trinket or two, but expect most of the memorabilia to be mass-produced fakes. (摩囉街; Upper Lascar Row, Sheung Wan; ⊙10am-6pm; ➌26)

Wan Kei Ho International Martial Arts Association MARTIAL ARTS

8 ◉ Map p30, C2

English-speaking Master Wan teaches northern Shaolin Kung Fu to a wide following of locals and foreigners. Classes are offered in the evenings from Monday to Thursday. Depending on how many classes you take, the monthly fees may range from HK$350 to HK$1600. (尹圻灝國際武術總會; ☏852 2544 1368, 852 9506 0075; www.kungfuwan.com; 3rd fl, Yue's House, 304 Des Voeux Rd Central, Sheung Wan; ⊙10am-8pm Mon-Fri, 9am-1pm Sat & Sun; Ⓜ Sheung Wan, exit A)

St John's Cathedral
CHURCH

9 Map p30, G4

Services have been held at this Anglican cathedral since it opened in 1849, with the exception of 1944, when the Japanese army used it as a social club. It suffered heavy damage during WWII, and the front doors were subsequently remade using timber salvaged from HMS *Tamar,* a British warship that guarded Victoria Harbour. You walk on sacred ground in more ways than one here: it is the only piece of freehold land in Hong Kong. Enter from Battery Path. (聖約翰座堂; ☑852 2523 4157; www.stjohnscathedral.org.hk; 4-8 Garden Rd, Central; admission free; ◷7am-6pm; ◻12A, 40, 40M, Ⓜ Central, exit K)

Two International Finance Centre
NOTABLE BUILDING

10 Map p30, F2

A pearl-coloured colossus resembling an electric shaver, this is the tallest building on Hong Kong Island. You can't get to the top, but you can get pretty high by visiting the Hong Kong Monetary Authority Information Centre. The building sits atop **IFC Mall** (☑852 2295 3308; www.ifc.com.hk; Ⓜ Hong Kong, exit F), which stretches to the lower levels of its sister building, the much-shorter **One IFC** (國際金融中心; One IFC; 1 Harbour View St, Central; Ⓜ Hong Kong, exit A2 or F). (國際金融中心; Two IFC; 8 Finance St, Central; Ⓜ Hong Kong, exit A2 or F)

Eating

City Hall Maxim's Palace
DIM SUM **$**

11 Map p30, G3

This 'palace' offers the quintessential Hong Kong dim sum experience. It's cheerful, it's noisy and it takes place in a huge kitschy hall with dragon decorations and hundreds of locals. A dizzying assortment of dim sum is paraded on trolleys the old-fashioned way. There's breakfast on Sunday from 9am, but people start queuing for a table at 8.30am. (美心皇宮; ☑852 2521 1303; 3rd fl, Lower Block, Hong Kong City Hall, 1 Edinburgh Pl, Central; meals from HK$150; ◷11am-3pm Mon-Sat, 9am-3pm Sun; 🛜🗶; Ⓜ Central, exit K)

Mrs Pound
ASIAN **$$**

12 Map p30, B2

On the outside, Mrs Pound looks like a traditional Sheung Wan stamp shop. But press the right stamp in the display window (hint: it glows) and a door

Top Tip
How Much?

HK$40 will buy you noodles and some greens, or a set meal at a fast-food chain.

A sit-down lunch in a midrange restaurant costs at least HK$80, and dinner HK$350. Dinner at upscale restaurants will set you back at least HK$600.

swings open to reveal a faux dive bar serving up cheeky twists on Asian street food. (☑852 3426 3949; www.mrspound.com; 6 Pound Lane, Sheung Wan; meals HK$150-400; ⏱noon-2.30pm & 5-11pm; Ⓜ Sheung Wan)

Chachawan
THAI $$

13 Map p30, B2

Specialising in the spicy cuisine of northeastern Thailand's Isaan region, this hip little spot is always jam-packed and plenty noisy. No curries or *pad thai* here, just scads of bright, herb-infused, chilli-packed salads (we like the green papaya with pork belly) and grilled fish and meat.

Cool your mouth with pinches of sticky rice, served in traditional rice baskets, and wash it all down with fusion-y cocktails incorporating Thai flavours such as sweet tea and lychee. No reservations – expect a wait at peak hours. (☑852 2549 0020; http://chachawan.hk; 206 Hollywood Rd, Sheung Wan; meals HK$200-450; ⏱12-2.30pm & 6.30pm-midnight; Ⓜ Sheung Wan, exit A2)

Pure Veggie House
VEGETARIAN, CHINESE $$

14 Map p30, E5

This Buddhist restaurant goes way beyond the usual tofu 'n' broccoli to serve innovative and delicious vegetarian dishes – fried rice with black truffle and pine nuts, seaweed-wrapped tofu rolls, and the city's best vegetarian Sichuan dishes prepared by its sister restaurant a few floors up, **San Xi Lou** (三希樓; ☑852 2838 8811; 7th fl Coda Plaza, 51 Garden Rd, Mid-Levels; meals HK$200-400; ⏱11am-10.30pm; 🚌12A from Admiralty MTR). Excellent all-veggie dim sum, served at lunch, will please even dedicated carnivores.

The decor resembles a rustic inn, with servers dressed in tunics like students in period dramas. (心齋; ☑852 2525 0556; 3rd fl, Coda Plaza, 51 Garden Rd, Mid-Levels; meals HK$250-500; ⏱10.30am-10.30pm; 🍴; 🚌12A from Admiralty MTR)

Caprice
MODERN FRENCH $$$

15 Map p30, F2

In contrast to its opulent decor, Caprice, with two Michelin stars, has a straightforward menu. The meals are masterfully crafted from ingredients flown in daily from France. The selections change, but experience says anything with duck, langoustine or pork belly is out of this world. Their artisanal cheeses, imported weekly, are the best you can get in Hong Kong. (☑852 3196 8888; www.fourseasons.com/hongkong; Four Seasons Hotel, 8 Finance St, Central; set lunch/dinner from HK$540/1740; ⏱noon-2.30pm & 6-10.30pm; 📶; Ⓜ Hong Kong, exit E1)

The Boss
CANTONESE $$$

16 Map p30, E3

Awarded one Michelin star, the Boss is a perfectionist. The flawless service, austere modern decor, and meticulous kitchen point to high expectations being imposed. The old-school Cantonese dishes are impressive, notably the deep-fried chicken pieces with home-fermented shrimp paste, and the baked-crab casserole. Dim sum, made with first-rate ingredients, is available at lunch. (波士廳; ☎852 2155 0552; www. theboss1.com; Basement, 58-62 Queen's Rd Central, Central; lunch/dinner sets from HK$230/680; ⏰11.30am-midnight Mon-Sat, from 11am Sun; 🛜; Ⓜ Central, exit D2)

Duddell's
CANTONESE $$$

Light Cantonese fare is served in riveting spaces (see **29** 🔒 Map p30, F4) enhanced by artwork – a graceful dining room awash in diffused light; a marble-tiled salon in modernised '50s chic; a leafy terrace. Saturday brunch (HK$680; noon to 3.30pm) with free-flowing champagne and all-you-can-eat dim sum is a welcome treat, especially given the usually petite serving portions. (都爹利會館; ☎852 2525 9191; www.duddells. co; Level 3 & 4 Shanghai Tang Mansion, 1 Duddell St, Central; lunch HK$500-800, dinner HK$800-1600; ⏰noon-2.30pm & 6-10.30pm Mon-Sat; 🛜; Ⓜ Central, exit G)

Lung King Heen
CANTONESE, DIM SUM $$$

17 Map p30, F2

The world's first Chinese restaurant to receive three Michelin stars still retains them. The Cantonese food, though by no means peerless in Hong Kong, is excellent in both taste and presentation, and when combined with the harbour views and the impeccable service, provides

PIDJ/SHUTTERSTOCK ©

'Ding Ding' (p34)

a truly stellar dining experience. The signature steamed lobster and scallop dumplings sell out early. (龍景軒; ☎852 3196 8888; www.fourseasons.com/hongkong; Four Seasons Hotel, 8 Finance St, Central; lunch HK$200-500, dinner HK$500-2000; ⏰noon-2.30pm & 6-10.30pm; 🛜; Ⓜ Hong Kong, exit E1)

Otto e Mezzo Bombana
ITALIAN $$$

18 Map p30, F3

Asia's only Italian restaurant with three Michelin stars lives up to its name, and Chef Bombana is here, sleeves rolled, to see that it does. 'Eight and a Half' is the place for white truffles, being the host of the local bidding for these pungent diamonds. To eat here though you'll need the tenacity of a truffle hound – book two months ahead. (☑852 2537 8859; www.ottoemezzobombana.com; Shop 202, 18 Chater Rd, Landmark Alexandra, Central; lunch/dinner from HK$700/1380; ⏱noon-2.30pm & 6.30-10.30pm Mon-Sat; ☎; Ⓜ Central, exit H)

Tim Ho Wan   DIM SUM $

| 19 | | Map p30, F2 |

Opened by a former Four Seasons chef, Tim Ho Wan was the first ever budget dim sum place to receive a Michelin star. Many relocations and branches later, the star is still tucked snugly inside their tasty titbits, including the top-selling baked barbecue pork bun. Expect to wait 15 to 40 minutes for a table. (添好運點心專門店; ☑852 2332 3078; www.timhowan.com; Shop 12a, Podium Level 1, 8 Finance St, IFC Mall, Central; dishes HK$50; ⏱9am-8.30pm; Ⓜ Hong Kong, exit E1)

Lin Heung
Tea House   CANTONESE, DIM SUM $

| 20 | | Map p30, D2 |

In the morning, this famous tea house is packed, just as it was in 1926, with older men reading newspapers. Dim sum (from HK$12), served from trolleys, is quickly snapped up, so hover near the kitchen if you want more choices.

The big bun and liver siu mai are coveted items, prized more for their nostalgic value than their taste. But the lotus-root patties and the braised stuffed duck (HK$150, advance booking required) live up to their reputation. (☑852 2544 4556; 160-164 Wellington St, Central; meals from HK$100; ⏱6am-11pm, dim sum to 3.30pm; Ⓜ Sheung Wan, exit E2)

Drinking

Cafe Deadend   CAFE

| 21 | | Map p30, B3 |

In Sheung Wan's leafy 'PoHo' neighbourhood of quiet boutiques and galleries, this tucked-away little cafe is one of the best places in Hong Kong to have a peaceful cup of coffee and read a book. (☑852 6716 7005; www.cafedeadend.com; 72 Po Hing Fong, Sheung Wan; meals HK$100-200; ⏱9.30am-6pm Tue-Sun; 🚌23, 40)

Sevva   COCKTAIL BAR

| 22 | | Map p30, F4 |

If there was a million-dollar view in Hong Kong, it'd be the one from the balcony of ultra-stylish Sevva – skyscrapers so close you can see their arteries of steel, with the harbour and Kowloon in the distance. At night it takes your breath away. To get there, though, you have to overcome expensive drinks and patchy service. (☑852 2537 1388; www.sevva.hk; 25th fl, Prince's Bldg, 10 Chater Rd, Central; ⏱noon-midnight Mon-Thu, to 2am Fri & Sat; ☎; Ⓜ Central, exit H)

Understand
Walls in Sheung Wan

In the 19th century many Chinese flocked to Hong Kong from the mainland in search of employment. The majority were coolies who settled in Sheung Wan. Afraid they'd get too close to the Europeans living nearby, the British imposed a segregation policy: Chinese to the west, Europeans to the east, with Aberdeen St serving as the invisible wall between the two. Conditions in the Chinese quarter were atrocious, and a bubonic plague broke out in 1894, killing 20,000.

From the time of the plague until after WWII, other walls were erected in Sheung Wan. To prevent landslides on steep Hong Kong Island, masonry workers shored up many slopes adjacent to main roads with stone retaining walls. Open joints between the stones allowed strong species such as Chinese banyans to sprout, further strengthening the walls. Today, Sheung Wan is one of Hong Kong's most cosmopolitan areas, but the 'wall trees' are still there.

Shopping

Queen's Road West Incense Shops
ARTS & CRAFTS

23 🔒 Map p30, A2

At 136–150 Queen's Rd West, there are shops selling incense and paper offerings for the dead. The latter are burned to propitiate departed souls and the choice of combustibles is mind-blowing – dim sum, iPad, Rolexes, Viagra tablets and – the latest – solar-powered water heaters. You may buy them as souvenirs, but remember that keeping these offerings meant for the dead (rather than burning them) is supposed to bring bad luck. (Queen's Rd W, Sheung Wan; ⏰8am-7pm; 🚌26)

Lam Kie Yuen Tea Co
FOOD & DRINKS

24 🔒 Map p30, C2

This shop, which has been around since 1955, is testament to just how much tea there is in China. From unfermented to fully fermented, and everything in between, there's simply too much to choose from. But don't panic – the owner will offer you a tasting. (林奇苑茶行; 📞852 2543 7145; www.lkytea.com; 105-107 Bonham Strand E, Sheung Wan; ⏰9am-6.30pm Mon-Sat; Ⓜ Sheung Wan, exit A2)

Chan Shing Kee
ANTIQUES

25 🔒 Map p30, D2

This shop with a three-storey showroom is run by Daniel Chan, the third generation of a family that's been in the business for 70 years. Chan Shing Kee is known to collectors and museums worldwide for its fine classical Chinese furniture (16th to 18th century).

Understand

British Colonisation & Its End

European traders began importing opium into Hong Kong in the 18th century, and by the start of the 19th century, the British were aggressively trading this 'foreign mud' for Chinese tea, silk and porcelain.

Opium Wars

China's attempts to end the opium trade gave Britain a pretext for military action; gunboats were sent in. In 1841 the Union Jack was hoisted on Hong Kong Island, and the Treaty of Nanking, which ended the First Opium War, ceded the island to the British crown. At the end of the Second Opium War in 1860, Britain took possession of Kowloon Peninsula, and in 1898 a 99-year lease was granted for the New Territories.

Transformation

Through the 20th century waves of refugees fled China for Hong Kong. Trade flourished, until the Japanese invasion in 1941. By the end of WWII Hong Kong's population had plummeted. But trouble in China again saw refugees push the population beyond 2 million. This, together with a UN trade embargo on China during the Korean War, enabled Hong Kong to reinvent itself as one of the world's most dynamic ports and manufacturing and financial-service centres.

Return of Sovereignty

Britain agreed to return Hong Kong to China in 1997, and on 1 July 1997, the British era ended.

In 2012 Leung Chun-ying became Hong Kong's fourth chief executive. Leung's pro-Beijing stance distresses many Hong Kongers, a sentiment exacerbated by the city's spiralling living costs and the influx of mainland tourists. Rising tensions with Běijīng dominate Hong Kong politics, putting the 'One Country, Two Systems' experiment in peril.

But despite the general mood of anxiety, all is not doom and gloom. If anything, these challenges are stirring a strong spirit among many people to defend the rule of law and their civil liberties.

Scholar's objects, such as ancient screens and wooden boxes, are also available. (陳勝記; ☎852 2543 1245; www.chanshingkee.com; 228-230 Queen's Rd Central, Sheung Wan; ⏰9am-6pm Mon-Sat; 🚌101, 104)

Gallery of the Pottery Workshop
ART, HOMEWARES

26 🔒 Map p30, D3

This gallery showcases playful ceramic objects made by local ceramic artists and artisans from the mainland and overseas. The lovely pieces range from crockery to sculptures. (樂天陶社; ☎852 9842 5889, 852 2525 7949; www.potteryworkshop.com.cn; 3rd fl Hollywood House, 27-29 Hollywood Rd, Soho; ⏰1-6pm Tue-Sun; 🚌26)

Armoury
CLOTHING

27 🔒 Map p30, F4

This elegant shop is a specialist in refined menswear sourced from around the world. Choose from tailored suits and a high-quality selection of shoes and ties to match. Ask about their bespoke suits and custom footwear. (☎852 2804 6991; www.thearmoury.com; 307 Pedder Bldg, 12 Pedder St, Central; ⏰11am-8pm Mon-Sat; Ⓜ Central, exit D1)

Picture This
GIFTS & SOUVENIRS

28 🔒 Map p30, F4

The vintage posters, photographs, prints, antiquarian books and antique maps of Hong Kong and Asia on sale here will appeal to collectors or anyone seeking an unusual gift. Prices are not cheap but they guarantee all maps and prints to be originals. (☎852 2525

Cat Street (p34)

2803; www.picturethiscollection.com; 13th fl, 9 Queen's Rd, Central; ⏰10am-7pm Mon-Sat, noon-5pm Sun; Ⓜ Central, exit H)

Shanghai Tang
CLOTHING, HOMEWARE

29 🔒 Map p30, F4

This elegant four-level store is the place to go if you fancy a body-hugging *qipao* (cheongsam) with a modern twist, a Chinese-style clutch or a lime-green mandarin jacket. Custom tailoring takes two weeks to a month and requires a fitting. It also stocks cushions, picture frames, teapots, even mah-jong tile sets, designed in a modern chinoiserie style. (上海灘; ☎852 2525 7333; www.shanghaitang.com; 1 Duddell St, Shanghai Tang Mansion, Central; ⏰10.30am-8pm; Ⓜ Central, exit D1)

APHOTOSTORY/SHUTTERSTOCK©

Top Sights
Victoria Peak

Getting There

🚌 Bus 15 from Central to the summit; bus 15C or 12S to Peak Tram Lower Terminus.

🚃 Peak Tram Lower Terminus, 33 Garden Rd, Central (single/return HK$28/40; every 10 to 15 minutes, 7am to midnight).

Standing at 552m, Victoria Peak is the highest point on Hong Kong Island. The Peak is also one of the most visited spots by tourists in Hong Kong, and it's not hard to see why. Sweeping views of the vibrant metropolis, verdant woods, easy but spectacular walks – all reachable in just eight minutes from Central.

Hong Kong skyline from Victoria Peak

Getting to the Top

The best way to reach the Peak is by the 125-year-old gravity-defying **Peak Tram** (Lower Terminus, 33 Garden Rd, Central; one way/return adult HK$28/40, child 3-11yr & seniors over 65yr HK$11/18; ⏲7am-midnight; Ⓜ Central, exit J2). Rising almost vertically above the high-rises nearby, Asia's oldest funicular clanks its way up the hillside to finish at the Peak Tower. The lower terminus in Central has an interesting gallery that houses a replica of the earliest carriage. The **Peak Galleria** (山頂廣場; 118 Peak Rd, Victoria Peak), adjoining the anvil-shaped **Peak Tower** (凌霄閣; ☎852 2849 0668; 128 Peak Rd, Victoria Peak; ⏲10am-11pm Mon-Fri, 8am-11pm Sat, Sun & public holidays), has an admission-free viewing deck, though its harbour views are obscured.

Exploring the Peak

Some 500m to the northwest of the upper terminus, up steep Mt Austin Rd, is the site of the old governor's summer lodge, which was burned to the ground by Japanese soldiers during WWII. The beautiful **gardens** remain, however, and have been refurbished with faux-Victorian gazebos and stone pillars. They are open to the public.

The dappled 3.5km circuit formed by Harlech Rd on the south, just outside the Peak Lookout, and Lugard Rd on the northern slope, which it runs into, takes about 45 minutes to cover. A further 2km along Peak Rd will lead you to Pok Fu Lam Reservoir Rd. Hatton Rd, reachable by Lugard or Harlech Rds, on the western slope goes all the way down to the University of Hong Kong. The 50km Hong Kong Trail also starts on the Peak.

維多利亞山頂

Map p30, C5

☎852 2522 0922

www.thepeak.com.hk

admission free

⏲24hr

☑ Top Tips

▶ If you don't want to pay the fee for the Peak Tower viewing deck, the Lion Pavilion – just east of the Peak Tram terminus – is the best place to get a free view of Victoria Harbour.

▶ The Peak Galleria has very good deals on souvenirs.

✗ Take a Break

▶ Grab a bite at the **Peak Lookout** (太平山餐廳; ☎852 2849 1000; www.peaklookout.com.hk; 121 Peak Rd, The Peak; lunch/dinner from HK$250/350; ⏲10.30am-11.30pm Mon-Fri, from 8.30am Sat & Sun), an international restaurant in a vintage building.

Explore

Hong Kong Island: Lan Kwai Fong & Soho

Lan Kwai Fong and Soho form the party epicentre of Hong Kong. Lan Kwai Fong is an alleyway dog-legging south and west from D'Aguilar St; as an area it also covers D'Aguilar St, Wo On Lane, Wing Wah Lane and Wyndham St. The crowd here is relatively young, middle-class and cosmopolitan. Soho ('south of Hollywood Rd') has art galleries and antique shops, plus bars and restaurants.

The Sights in a Day

Take the Peak Tram up to **Victoria Peak** (p42) and spend two hours there. Back down, have dim sum amidst nostalgic splendour at Michelin-crowned **Luk Yu Tea House** (p52).

Browse the art galleries and antique shops on Hollywood Rd, taking care not to miss the **Central Police Station** (p49). Design hub **PMQ** (p50) is good for modern souvenirs. Break for tea at 1950s style **Lan Fong Yuen** (p52) or raw food haven **Mana!** (p51).

Muscles sore from walking? Go for a body or foot massage at **Happy Foot Reflexology** (p51). Getting kneaded works up an appetite: feast on old Cantonese dishes at **Ser Wong Fun** (p52). Spend the rest of the night bar crawling.

For a local's day in Lan Kwai Fong & Soho, see p46.

Local Life
LKF & Soho Bar Crawl (p46)

Best of Hong Kong

Eating
Luk Yu Tea House (p52)

Dumpling Yuan (p51)

Lan Fong Yuen (p52)

Drinking
Club 71 (p47)

Angel's Share Whisky Bar (p54)

Shopping
Grotto Fine Art (p58)

PMQ (p59)

G.O.D. (p57)

Getting There

🚌 **Bus** 26 runs along Hollywood Rd.

Ⓜ **Metro** Central station (Island and Tsuen Wan lines).

Local Life
LKF & Soho Bar Crawl

Here are some of the more charismatic venues in Lan Kwai Fong (LKF) and Soho favoured by seasoned revellers. While some may appeal to wine connoisseurs, others to cocktail or culture buffs, all of the selections command enough charm, booze and atmosphere to give anyone a memorable (even if not fully remembered) night out.

❶ Clubby Cocktails

Stockton (☎852 2565 5268; www.stockton.com.hk; 32 Wyndham St, Lan Kwai Fong; ⏱6pm-late Mon-Sat; Ⓜ Central, exit D2) evokes the ambience of a private club in Victorian London. Chesterfield sofas and the odd candelabra are arranged to form intimate niches for sipping the rum- and whisky-based cocktails. Make a reservation if coming after 9pm on a weekend.

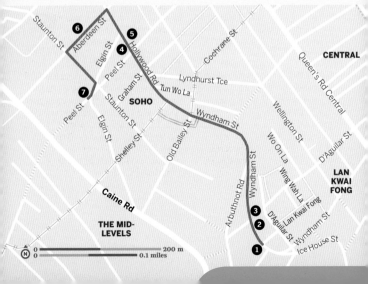

❷ Play Ball While You Drink

Tazmania Ballroom (☎852 2801 5009; www.tazmaniaballroom.com; 1st fl, LKF Tower, 33 Wyndham St, Lan Kwai Fong; ⏰5pm-late, happy hour 5-8pm; Ⓜ Central, exit D2) whips out ping-pong tables every Tuesday, Thursday and Saturday. The dress code, however, is casual glam, not Chinese national team. You can shoot pool with bankers or take a breather on the balcony.

❸ Chill, Frolic, Repeat

Sophisticated **Tivo Bar** (☎852 2116 8055; www.aqua.com.hk; 43-55 Wyndham St, Lan Kwai Fong; ⏰6pm-midnight Sun-Thu, to late Fri & Sat; Ⓜ Central, exit D2) delights with open frontage, aperitivo-type snacks and an exuberant crowd. On the first and third Sunday of the month, lovely hostesses in drag take over from 7pm and whip up the action for the Tivo Tea Dance.

❹ A Herbal Detox

Kung Lee (公利真料竹蔗水; ☎852 2544 3571; 60 Hollywood Rd, Soho; juice from HK$11; ⏰11am-11pm; 🚌26) has been selling herbal teas and fresh sugarcane juice since 1948 – the quality is unchanged, as are the charming vintage tiles. There's 'turtle jelly' too, made with the powdered shell of a certain type of turtle – good for detoxing on your way to the next bar.

❺ Meet Local Activists

Named after a protest on 1 July 2003 against an article that would limit freedom of speech, **Club 71** (Basement, 67 Hollywood Rd, Soho; ⏰3pm-2am Mon-Sat, 6pm-1am Sun, happy hour 3-9pm; 🚌26, Ⓜ Central, exit D1) is where activists and artists gather for beer and blues-jamming. Out front is the location where revolutionaries plotted to overthrow the Qing dynasty a century ago. Enter the alley at 67 Hollywood Rd.

❻ Swinging '60s

Tai Lung Fung (☎852 2572 2886; 1st fl, shop H107, PMQ, 35 Aberdeen St, Central; ⏰11am-11pm; Ⓜ Sheung Wan) rocks a retro 1960s Hong Kong vibe, with a tiled bar and vintage public works posters. An arty crowd sips homebrewed liqueurs in flavours such as osmanthus and pǔ'ěr tea, while attacking plates of old-school nibbles including shrimp toast.

❼ Craft Beer on Tap

Roundhouse Taproom (☎852 2366 4880; www.roundhouse.com.hk; 62 Peel St, Soho; ⏰noon-11pm, happy hour noon-8pm; Ⓜ Central, exit D1) has some of the best craft beer on tap – 25 varieties, including limited edition beers. Pick your brew from the iPad menu and savour it inside the brightly lit bar or on the steps just outside.

Central–Mid-Levels Escalator

Sights

Central–Mid-Levels Escalator

LANDMARK

1 ◎ Map p48, B3

The world's longest covered outdoor people-mover zigzags from Central's offices to homes near Conduit Rd. Embark and let the streets unveil themselves – Stanley and Wellington with their glamour and tradition; Gage and Lyndhurst where florists and prostitutes once hawked their wares; Hollywood, Hong Kong's second oldest street; Staunton, whose porcelain shops made way for Soho; then Shelley, named unromantically after an infamous auditor-general. (🕑 down 6-10am, up 10.30am-midnight)

Central Police Station

HISTORIC BUILDING

2 ◎ Map p48, C3

Built between 1841 and 1919, Hong Kong's oldest symbol of law and order is this now-disused, police-magistracy-prison complex modelled after London's Old Bailey. The large compound is currently being redeveloped into an arts hub with cinema, museum and boutique shopping mall. (10 Hollywood Rd, Lan Kwai Fong; 🚌 26, Ⓜ Central, exit D2)

PMQ

PMQ

ARTS CENTRE

3 ◎ Map p48, A2

This new arts hub occupies the modernist buildings and breezy courtyard of the old married police quarters (c 1951). Dozens of small galleries and shops hawk hip hand-made jewellery, leather goods, prints, clothing, housewares and more, making the PMQ a terrific place to hunt for non-tacky souvenirs. There are also several restaurants and bak-eries, and a large exhibit space with a rotating variety of free shows. (元 創方; ☎852 2870 2335; www.pmq.org.hk; S614, Block A, PMQ, 35 Aberdeen St, Soho;

⏱building open 7am-11pm, most shops open noon-8pm; ☐26, Ⓜ Central, exit D2)

Flawless Hong Kong

SPA

4 ◎ Map p48, D4

This award-winning spa attracts a youngish clientele with its homey setting and vast array of no-nonsense treatments for the face (from HK$580 up) and nails (manicures from HK$160). They use sophisticated 'age-combating' serums, but nothing too airy-fairy such as flowers or pebbles. (☎852 2869 5868; www.flawless.hk.com; 4th fl, Sea Bird House, 22-28 Wyndham St, Lan Kwai Fong; ⏱10am-10pm; Ⓜ Central, exit D1)

Happy Foot Reflexology Centre

SPA

5 🎯 Map p48, D4

Getting intense, Chinese-style foot massages is a regular treat for many hard-driving Hong Kong business people. Foot/body massage starts at HK$200/250 for 50 minutes at this popular reflexology spa. (知足樂; 📞 852 2522 1151; www.happyfoot.hk; 19th & 20th fl, Century Sq, 1 D'Aguilar St, Lan Kwai Fong; ⏰ 10am-midnight; Ⓜ Central, exit D2)

Eating

Ho Lee Fuk

MODERN CHINESE $$

6 🍴 Map p48, A2

As irreverent as its name suggests, this buzzy underground spot does a winkingly modern take on retro Chinatown cuisine. Prawn toasts are served with a dollop of Kewpie mayo and savoury bonito flakes, the *char siu* is upmarket with Kurobuta pork, and prawn *lo mein* is spangled with crunchy bits of fried garlic and slicked with shellfish oil. The atmosphere is very see-and-be-seen, despite nightclub-level darkness. (📞 852 2810 0860; http://holeefookhk.tumblr.com/; 1-5 Elgin St, Soho; meals HK$250-500; ⏰ 6-11pm Sun-Thu, to midnight Fri & Sat; Ⓜ Central, exit D2)

Mana! Fast Slow Food

VEGAN $

7 🍴 Map p48, C3

A vegan and raw food haven that whips up smoothies, salads and desserts for the professional crowd. Flat breads (available gluten-free) are baked in-shop by the cheerful staff then smothered with organic veggies and Mediterranean dips. Besides tasty, guilt-free food, Mana offers a hippy vibe that makes one forget its physical smallness and not-so-bohemian prices. (📞 852 2851 1611; www.mana.hk; 92 Wellington St, Soho; meals HK$100-200; ⏰ 10am-10pm; 📶 ✍; Ⓜ Central, exit D2)

Dumpling Yuan

DUMPLING $

8 🍴 Map p48, C2

Locals and visitors from the north flock to this little shop for its nine varieties of juicy bundles of heaven, more commonly known as lamb and cumin, pork and chives, egg and tomato or vegetarian dumplings. (餃子園; 📞 852 2541 9737; 98 Wellington St, Soho; meals from HK$40; ⏰ 11am-10.30pm Mon-Sat; ✍; 🚇 40M)

Kau Kee Restaurant

NOODLES $

9 🍴 Map p48, A1

You can argue till the noodles go soggy about whether Kau Kee has the best beef brisket in town. Whatever the verdict, the meat – served with toothsome noodles in a fragrant beefy broth – is hard to beat. During the 90 years of the shop's existence, film stars and politicians have joined the queue for a table. (九記牛腩; ☎852 2850 5967; 21 Gough St, Sheung Wan; meals from HK$40; ⏰12.30-7.15pm & 8.30-11.30pm Mon-Sat; Ⓜ Sheung Wan, exit E2)

Luk Yu Tea House
CANTONESE $$

11 Map p48, D3

This gorgeous teahouse (c 1933), known for its masterful cooking and Eastern art-deco decor, was the haunt of opera artists, writers and painters (including the creator of one exorbitant ink-and-brush gracing a wall) who came to give recitals and discuss the national fate. The food is old-school Cantonese fare such as sweet-and-sour pork, prawn toast and a variety of dim-sum dumplings and pastries. (陸羽茶室; ☎852 2523 5464; 24-26 Stanley St, Lan Kwai Fong; meals HK$300; ⏰7am-10pm, dim sum to 5.30pm; ✈; Ⓜ Central, exit D2)

Top Tip
Booking & Tipping

It's strongly advisable to book ahead in all but the cheapest restaurants, especially on Friday and Saturday nights. Most places above midrange add a 10% service charge to the bill. If the service at a top-end restaurant is outstanding, you might consider adding another 5% or 10% on top of the service charge. At midrange places, HK$5 to HK$20 is sufficient.

Lan Fong Yuen
CAFE $

11 Map p48, B3

This rickety facade hides an entire *cha chaan tang* (tea cafe). Lan Fong Yuen (1952) is believed to be the inventor of the 'pantyhose' milk tea. Over a thousand cups of the strong and silky brew are sold daily alongside pork-chop buns, tossed noodles and other hasty tasties. Watch staff work their magic while you wait for a table. (蘭芳園; ☎852 2544 3895, 852 2854 0731; 2 & 4A Gage St, Soho; meals from HK$60, cover charge HK$20; ⏰7am-6pm Mon-Sat; 🚇5B)

Mak's Noodle
NOODLES, CANTONESE $

12 Map p48, C2

At this legendary shop noodles are made the traditional way with a bamboo pole and served perched on a spoon placed over the bowl so they won't go soggy. The beef brisket noodles are remarkable. (麥奀雲吞麵世家; ☎852 2854 3810; 77 Wellington St, Soho; noodles HK$32-48; ⏰11am-8pm; 🚇40M)

Ser Wong Fun
CANTONESE $

13 Map p48, C3

This snake-soup specialist whips up old Cantonese dishes that are as tantalising as its celebrated broth, and the packed tables attest to it. Many regulars come just for the homemade pork-liver sausage infused with rose wine – perfect over a bowl of immaculate white rice, on a red tablecloth. Booking advised. (蛇王芬; ☎852 2543 1032; 30 Cochrane St, Soho; meals HK$70; ⏰11am-10.30pm; Ⓜ Central, exit D1)

Steamed dim sum buns and dumplings

Tai Cheong Bakery BAKERY $

14 🍴 Map p48, B3

Tai Cheong was best known for its lighter-than-air beignets (deep-fried dough rolled in sugar; *sa yung* in Cantonese) until former governor Chris Patten was photographed wolfing down its egg-custard tarts. Since then 'Fat Patten' egg tarts have hogged the limelight. (泰昌餅家; 📞852 8300 8301; 35 Lyndhurst Tce, Central; pastries from HK$8; ⏰7.30am-9pm Mon-Sat, 8.30am-9pm Sun; 🚍40M)

Yue Hing STREET FOOD $

15 🍴 Map p48, C2

One of a gang of *dai pai dong* (food stalls) earmarked for preservation, easygoing Yue Hing reinvents the Hong Kong sandwich by topping the usual suspects (ham, spam and egg) with peanut butter and cooked cabbage. And it works! Allow 15 minutes for preparation as these wacky wedges are made to order. (裕興; 76-78 Stanley St, Soho; meals HK$25-40; ⏰8.15am-2pm; Ⓜ️Central, exit D2)

Dragon-i

Drinking

Angel's Share Whisky Bar   BAR

16 🚇 Map p48, C3

One of Hong Kong's best whisky bars,
this clubby place has over 100 whiskies
from the world over – predominantly
Scottish, but also French, Japanese and
American. One of these, a 23-year-old
Macallan, comes straight out of a large
180L oak barrel placed in the centre
of the room. If you're hungry, there's
a selection of whisky-inspired dishes.
(📞852 2805 8388; www.angelsshare.hk; 2nd
fl, Amber Lodge, 23 Hollywood Rd, Lan Kwai
Fong; ⏰3pm-2am Mon-Thu, to 3am Fri & Sat;
Ⓜ Central, exit D1)

Studio   LOUNGE

17 🚇 Map p48, D4

The house jazz band fires up every
night at 9pm at this 1950s-inspired
jazz lounge in Lan Kwai Fong. Warm
wood walls and dramatic lighting
give the open space a glamorous, theatrical vibe. Post-band DJs spin until
late, late, late. Cocktails are pricey,
but the whisky menu is one of the
better ones around. (www.studioclub.
asia; 1st fl, On Hing Bldg, 1 On Hing Tce,
Central; ⏰6pm-4am; Ⓜ Central, exit D2)

LONELY PLANET/GETTY IMAGES ©

Dragon-i
BAR, CLUB

18 Map p48, C4

This fashionable venue has both an in-door bar and a terrace over Wyndham St filled with caged songbirds. Go after midnight and watch Ukrainian models and Cantopop stars sipping Krug and air kissing, as DJs fill the dance floor with hip hop, R&B and jazz. Go early or dress to kill if you want to be let in. (☏852 3110 1222; www.dragon-i.com.hk; upper ground fl, the Centrium, 60 Wyndham St, Lan Kwai Fong; ⊙noon-late, terrace happy hour 3-9pm Mon-Sat; ➁26, Ⓜ Central, exit D2)

Globe
PUB

19 Map p48, B3

Besides an impressive list of 150 imported beers, including 13 on tap, the Globe serves T8, the first cask-conditioned ale brewed in Hong Kong. Occupying an enviable 370 sq metres, the bar has a huge dining area with long wooden tables and comfortable banquettes. It's also popular for its very decent British pub grub. (☏852 2543 1941; www.theglobe.com.hk; 45-53 Graham St, Soho; ⊙10am-2am, happy hour 10am-8pm; Ⓜ Central, exit D1)

Quinary
COCKTAIL BAR

20 Map p48, A2

A sleek, moodily-lit cocktail bar, Quinary attracts a well-dressed crowd to sip Asian-inspired cocktail creations such as the Quinary Sour (whisky, licorice root, Chinese black sugar), the Oolong Tea Collins (vodka, oolong tea cordial) or the Checkers (vodka, black sesame syrup, vanilla ice cream). Prices are high, making this a good place to start the evening before moving on to cheaper and less elegant environs. (☏852 2851 3223; www.quinary. hk; 56-58 Hollywood Rd, Soho; ⊙5pm-2am Mon-Sat; Ⓜ Central exit D2)

T:ME
GAY

21 Map p48, B2

This small, chic gay bar is located in a residential back alley facing a small park; drinks are a bit on the pricey side but it has happy hour through-out the week. Enter through the alley off Peel St just north of Hollywood Rd. (☏852 2332 6565; www.time-bar.com; 65 Hollywood Rd, Soho; ⊙6pm-2am Mon-Sat; Ⓜ Central, exit D1)

☑ Top Tip

Stubbed Out

All indoor areas of eateries are now smoke-free. The ban does not apply to unsheltered outdoor spaces of bars and restaurants. Some bars, however, will risk get-ting fined in order to attract more customers. You know which ones they are by the ashtray noncha-lantly left on tables.

Smoking is also banned in shopping malls, cinemas, muse-ums, public transport, as well as beaches and parks.

Entertainment

Senses 99　　LIVE MUSIC

22 ⭐ Map p48, B2

This two-floor speakeasy inside a pre-WWII building has all the features of a tasteful mid-century residence – high ceilings, balconies overlooking a quiet street, folding screen doors and distressed couches. Music sessions begin after 10pm, but before that you can take charge of the drum set and electric guitar on the 3rd floor to start a jam session or join one. (☑852 9466 2675; www. sense99.com; 2nd & 3rd fl, 99 Wellington St, Soho; ⏰9pm-late Fri & Sat; Ⓜ Sheung Wan, exit E2)

Ⓠ Local Life
LGBT Resources

Hong Kong has a small but vibrant and growing gay-and-lesbian scene and the annual **Pride Parade** in November now attracts rainbow flag-wavers by the thousands.

Contact **Pink Alliance** (http://pinkalliance.hk) for information about LGBTQ culture and events in Hong Kong. Or check out the latest events in Hong Kong's first free gay lifestyle magazine, *Dim Sum Magazine* (www.dimsum-hk.com).

Les Peches (☑852 9101 8001; lespechesinfo@yahoo.com) is Hong Kong's premier lesbian organisation has monthly events for lesbians, bisexual women and their friends.

Fringe Club　　LIVE MUSIC, THEATRE

23 ⭐ Map p48, D5

The Fringe, housed in a Victorian building (c 1892) that was part of a dairy farm, offers original music in the Dairy several nights a week, with jazz, rock and world music getting the most airplay. The intimate theatres host eclectic local and international performances. The Fringe sits on the border of Lan Kwai Fong. (藝穗會; ☑theatre bookings 852 2521 9126, 852 2521 7251; www.hkfringe. com.hk; 2 Lower Albert Rd, Lan Kwai Fong; ⏰noon-midnight Mon-Thu, to 3am Fri & Sat; Ⓜ Central, exits D1, D2 & G)

Peel Fresco　　JAZZ

24 ⭐ Map p48, A2

Charming Peel Fresco has live jazz six nights a week, with local and overseas acts performing on a small but spectacular stage next to teetering faux-Renaissance paintings. The action starts around 9.30pm, but get there at 9pm to secure a seat. (☑852 2540 2046; www.peelfresco.com; 49 Peel St, Soho; ⏰5pm-late Mon-Sat; 🚍13, 26, 40M)

TakeOut Comedy Club　　COMEDY

25 ⭐ Map p48, A3

In need of some LOL? Hong Kong's first full-time comedy club, founded by Chinese-American Jameson Gong, has stand-up and improv acts in English, Cantonese and Mandarin. It also hosts visiting comedians from overseas. See website for program.

(☏852 6220 4436; www.takeoutcomedy. com; Basement, 34 Elgin St, Soho; 🚇26)

Shopping

Arch Angel Antiques

ANTIQUES

26 Map p48, B2

Though the specialities are ancient porcelain and tombware, Arch Angel packs a lot more into its three floors: it has everything from mah-jong sets and terracotta horses to palatial furniture. (☏852 2851 6848; 53-55 Hollywood Rd, Lan Kwai Fong; ⏰9.30am-6.30pm Mon-Sat, to 6pm Sun; 🚇26)

Fang Fong Projects

CLOTHING

27 Map p48, A3

Wu Lai-fan's very wearable dresses are a clever mix of vintage fabric and 1980s silhouettes. The shop also carries some of her own designs. (69 Peel St, Lan Kwai Fong; ⏰11am-8pm Sun-Thu, noon-9pm Fri & Sat; 🚇26)

Flow

BOOKS

28 Map p48, B3

A sprawling jumble of second-hand English titles covers almost every inch of Flow. You'll need some patience to find whatever you're seeking; alternatively, let the friendly owner, Lam Sum, guide you to the

Top Tip

What's On & Tickets

Urbtix (www.urbtix.hk) and **Hong Kong Ticketing** (www.hkticketing. com) have tickets to every major event in Hong Kong. You can book through them or purchase tickets at the performance venues.

Artmap (www.artmap.com.hk)

Artslink (www.hkac.org.hk)

Time Out (www.timeout.com.hk)

right shelf. (☏852 2964 9483, 852 9278 5664; www.flowbooks.net; 7th fl, 1A Wing On Bldg, 38 Hollywood Rd, Lan Kwai Fong; ⏰noon-7pm; 🚇26)

G.O.D.

GIFTS, HOUSEWARES

29 Map p48, B3

Goods of Desire – or G.O.D. – is a cheeky local lifestyle brand, selling housewares, clothes, books and gifts with retro Hong Kong themes. Fun gets include aprons printed with images of Hong Kong's famous neon signs, strings of fairy lights resembling the red lampshades ubiquitous in Hong Kong wet markets, and bed linen with themes like koi fish, vintage Hong Kong mailboxes or double happiness signs. (Goods of Desire; ☏852 2805 1876; http://god.com.hk/; 48 Hollywood Rd, Soho; ⏰11am-9pm)

Arch Angel Antiques (p57)

Grotto Fine Art

ART

30 🔒 Map p48, D5

This exquisite gallery, founded by a scholar in Hong Kong art, is one of very few that represents predominantly local artists. The small but excellent selection of works shown ranges from painting and sculpture to ceramics and mixed media. Prices are reasonable too. (嘉圖; 🕿 852 2121 2270; www.grottofineart.com; 2nd fl, 31C-D

Wyndham St, Lan Kwai Fong; ⏱11am-7pm Mon-Sat; Ⓜ Central, exit D2)

Karin Weber Gallery

ANTIQUES

31 🔒 Map p48, A2

Karin Weber has an interesting mix of Chinese country antiques and contemporary Asian artwork. She is able to arrange antique-buying trips to Guǎngdōng for serious buyers. (🕿 852 2544 5004; www.karinwebergallery.com; 20 Aberdeen St, Soho; ⏱11am-7pm Tue-Sat, by appointment Sun; 🚌26)

Lam Gallery

ANTIQUES

32 🔒 Map p48, B2

Arguably the best shop in the area for sculptures, this is the largest of several stores owned by the Lam family on Hollywood Rd. Sculpted pieces from the Neolithic period to the Qing dynasty predominate. Other products include ceramics, bronze, paintings, gold and silverware. Lam is known by collectors and auction dealers worldwide, and offers restoration services. (松心閣; ☎852 2554 4666; 61 Hollywood Rd, Lan Kwai Fong; ⏱10.30am-6.30pm Mon-Fri, 11am-6pm Sat; 🚇26, Ⓜ Central, exit D2)

Linva Tailor

FASHION & ACCESSORIES

33 🔒 Map p48, C3

Fancy a *cheongsam* aka *qipao* (body-hugging Chinese dress)? Bring your own silk or choose from the selection here. If you're pushed for time, the bespoke tailors, Mr and Mrs Leung, are happy to mail the completed items to you. (年華時裝公司; ☎852 2544 2456; 38 Cochrane St, Soho; ⏱9.30am-6.30pm Mon-Sat; 🚇26)

PMQ

HANDICRAFTS, JEWELLERY

The modernist building (see 3 👁) Map p48, A2) that was once the police married quarters is now one of the best places in Hong Kong to shop for pieces by local designers, jewellery makers and artisans, with dozens of shops and boutiques occupying the old apartments. Top picks include the hip streetwear of Kapok, Hong Kong-themed gifts at HKTDC Design Gallery, industrially inspired jewellery at The Little Finger, and bamboo kitchenware at Bamboo Home. (☎852 2870 2335; www.pmq.org.hk; 35 Aberdeen St, Central; ⏱most shops 11am-7pm)

Wattis Fine Art

ANTIQUES

34 🔒 Map p48, B3

This upstairs gallery has a great collection of antique maps for sale. The selection of old photographs of Hong Kong and Macau is also impressive. Enter from Old Bailey St. (www.wattis.com.hk; 2nd fl, 20 Hollywood Rd, Lan Kwai Fong; ⏱10.30am-6pm Mon-Sat; 🚇26)

Explore

Hong Kong Island: Admiralty, Wan Chai & Causeway Bay

Quiet Admiralty offers class over quantity, whether it be shopping, sights or dining. To its east, Wan Chai is a seat of culture, a showcase for folk traditions and a nightlife guru, not to mention Hong Kong's most versatile kitchen. In the shopping hub of Causeway Bay, restaurants and department stores jockey for space with a racecourse and a cemetery.

The Sights in a Day

☀ Pay a leisurely 2½-hour visit to **Hong Kong Park** (p64) and the **Asia Society Hong Kong Centre** (p71). Stroll through Pacific Place mall, browsing the shops, as you make your way back downhill. Lunch on Cantonese barbecue at **Joy Hing** (p72).

☀ Spend two hours exploring the 'old Wan Chai' area, taking care not to miss **Pak Tai Temple** (p70), **Hung Shing Temple** (p70), the **Blue House** (p70) cluster, and the markets. Continue your journey north to Hennessy Rd, shopping for gadgets at the **Wan Chai Computer Centre** (p67) and soaking up the vibes at **Southorn Playground** (p66). Then tram it to Causeway Bay to shop in the malls and Caroline Haven (p73).

☾ Feast on Cantonese homecooking at **Fortune Kitchen** (p72), but leave stomach space for the tailor-made desserts of **Atum Desserant** (p72).

For a local's day in Admiralty, Wan Chai & Causeway Bay, see p66.

👁 Top Sights

Happy Valley Racecourse (p62)

Hong Kong Park (p64)

🔍 Local Life

Wan Chai Breather (p66)

♥ Best of Hong Kong

Eating
Fortune Kitchen (p72)

Seventh Son (p73)

Atum Desserant (p72)

Drinking
Tai Lung Fung (p75)

Myhouse (p76)

Elephant Grounds (p76)

Stone Nullah Tavern (p77)

Getting There

Ⓜ **Metro** Admiralty, Wan Chai, Causeway Bay and Tin Hau stations.

🚋 **Tram** East along Queensway, Johnston Rd and Hennessy Rd.

🚌 **Bus** Admiralty bus station below Queensway Plaza for buses around Hong Kong Island; buses 5, 5B and 26 for Yee Wo St (Causeway Bay).

Top Sights
Happy Valley Racecourse

Horse racing is Hong Kong's most popular spectator sport, and an evening at the races is one of the quintessential Hong Kong things to do. Every Wednesday from September to June, the Happy Valley Racecourse comes alive with eight electrifying races and an accompanying carnival of food and wine. You can try your hand at betting, or simply enjoy the collective exhilaration, the smell of the turf and the thunder of iron hoofs.

跑馬地馬場

◉ Map p69, G5

☎ 852 2895 1523

www.hkjc.com

2 Sports Rd, Happy Valley

HK$10

🕒 7-10.30pm Wed Sep-Jun

🚃 Happy Valley

How to Place a Bet

Pick up a betting slip and provide information on the type of bet and the amount you're betting (minimum is HK$10). Hand the slip and cash to staff at the back of the stands. You'll get a receipt, which you must show to claim your winnings after the race. Basic betting types include the following:

Win – you back one horse; it wins.

Place – your horse finishes first, second or third.

Quinella – your two chosen horses come first and second, in either order.

Quinella place – you back any two of the first three horses.

Tierce – you choose the first three horses in correct order.

Trio – like the tierce, but in any order.

Tours

For a full-on experience, join the **Come Horseracing Tour** (☏852 2368 7111, reservations 852 2316 2151; http://entertainment.hkjc.com/entertainment; per person from HK$1080), run during race meetings. Lasting 5 1/2 hours for night races and 7 hours for day races, the tour includes pick-up, admission to the Jockey Club members' area, buffet and a guided tour of the parade ring and the winning post.

Racing Museum

Racing buffs can visit the **Hong Kong Racing Museum** (☏852 2966 8065; 2nd fl, Happy Valley Stand, Wong Nai Chung Rd, Happy Valley; admission free; ☺noon-7pm, to 9pm race days) which showcases the lives of celebrated trainers, jockeys and horses, and key races over the past 150 years.

☑ Top Tips

▶ Avoid crowds by leaving just before the last race. Turn right as you leave the turnstiles and walk 10 minutes to the Causeway Bay MTR station at Times Sq.

✖ Take a Break

There's decent but over-priced pizza and kebabs at the racecourse, in addition to the offerings of a fast food outlet. But if you head some ways towards Causeway Bay, **Yu** (渝酸辣粉; ☏852 2838 8198; 4 Yiu Wa St, Causeway Bay; meals from HK$100; ☺noon-5pm & 6-11pm; Ⓜ Causeway Bay, exit A) awaits with chewy Sichuan noodles and flavour-packed dishes.

Top Sights
Hong Kong Park

Hong Kong Park is one of the most unusual parks in the world, emphasising creations such as its fountain plaza, conservatory, artificial ponds and waterfalls (a favourite of the newly-weds from the marriage registry within the park), children's playground and taichi garden. For all its artifice, the 8-hectare park is beautiful and, with a wall of skyscrapers on one side and mountains on the other, makes for dramatic photographs.

香港公園

👁 Map p68, A3

📞 852 2521 5041

www.lcsd.gov.hk/parks/hkp

19 Cotton Tree Dr, Admiralty

admission free, 🚻

🕑 park 6am-11pm

Ⓜ Admiralty, exit C1

Edward Youde Aviary

This **aviary** (尤德觀鳥園; Hong Kong Park, Admiralty; ⏱9am-5pm) is the highlight of the park. Designed like a rainforest, it has a wooden bridge suspended 10m above the ground, eye level with tree branches. The **Forsgate Conservatory** (霍士傑溫室; 10 Cotton Tree Dr, Admiralty; admission free; ⏱9am-5pm), on the slope overlooking the park, is the largest in Southeast Asia.

Flagstaff House Museum of Tea Ware

At the park's northernmost tip is this exquisite museum (旗桿屋茶具文物館; ☎852 2869 0690; www.lcsd.gov.hk/CE/Museum; 10 Cotton Tree Dr, Admiralty; admission free; ⏱10am-6pm Wed-Mon). Built in 1846 as the home of the commander of the British forces, Flagstaff House is the oldest colonial building in Hong Kong still standing in its original spot. Its Greek Revival elegance is complemented by the graceful tea ware from the 11th to the 20th century on show – bowls, brewing trays, sniffing cups, and teapots made of porcelain or purple clay.

KS Lo Gallery

The **KS Lo Gallery** (羅桂祥茶藝館; ☎852 2869 0690; 10 Cotton Tree Dr, Admiralty; admission free; ⏱10am-6pm Wed-Mon), in a building southeast of the museum, contains rare Chinese ceramics from famous kilns in ancient China and stone seals collected by the gallery's eponymous benefactor.

☑ **Top Tips**

▶ Lock Cha Tea Shop (p74) has talks on tea, as well as tea appreciation and calligraphy classes on weekdays. See the website and call them for details.

✖ **Take a Break**

▶ Recharge over tea and vegetarian dim sum at classy Lock Cha Tea Shop (p74). Book ahead if going for lunch or dinner.

Local Life
Wan Chai Breather

Wan Chai has plenty of places where residents or office workers go for a breather – not only parks, cafes and the usual suspects, but also unlikely havens where people can let off steam or zone out before checking back into the world. To visitors, these eclectic spaces offer a glimpse into some of the lesser seen facets of local society.

❶ Southorn Playground

Seniors come to this **playground** (修頓球場; Hennessy Rd, Wan Chai; ⊘6am-11.30pm; Ⓜ Wan Chai, exit A3) to play chess, and students to shoot hoops and kick ball. There are hip-hop dance-offs, housewives shaking a leg, outreach social workers and a trickle of lunchers. This playground marks the boundary between home and

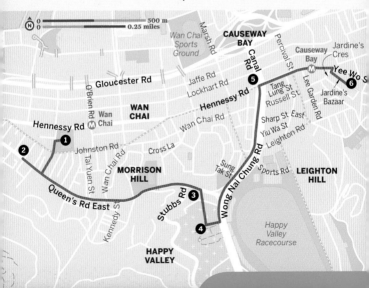

play – between Wan Chai's red-light district of yore and the residential area. Rumour has it that in the 1950s, sailors visiting 'Suzy Wong' bars (hostess bars popularised by the 1960 movie *The World of Suzy Wong* starring Nancy Kwan) would never venture beyond this playground, no matter how drunk.

② Gadget Shopping

Between appointments, office workers pack themselves into this **Wan Chai Computer Centre** (p80) next to Southorn Playground, sometimes just so they can have their finger on the gadgetry pulse. It's got everything from iPhones to custom-made 'white box' computers. You'll need to jostle with the locals for a good look at the price tags though. There's little leeway for bargaining.

③ Khalsa Diwan Sikh Temple

This **temple** (☑852 2572 4459; www.khalsadiwan.com; 371 Queen's Rd E, Wan Chai; ⏰5am-8pm; ⊡10) in blue and white was built in 1901, and extends its services to any caste, colour or creed. Sunday prayer (9am to 1pm) sees 1000 believers and non-believers in worship; fewer at the daily prayers (4am to 8am, 6pm to 8pm). It also hands out free vegetarian meals (11.30am to 8.30pm).

④ Hong Kong Cemetery

Nearby, opposite the racecourse, this crowded Protestant **cemetery** (香港墳場; www.fehd.gov.hk/english/cc/introduction.html; Wong Nai Chung Rd, Happy Valley; ⏰7am-6pm or 7pm; 🛗; Ⓜ Causeway Bay, exit A) lies alongside the Jewish, Hindu, Muslim and Catholic cemeteries of Hong Kong. Tombstones date to the mid-1800s and include those of tycoons, colonialists and actresses.

⑤ Rent-a-Curse Grannies

Under the Canal Rd flyover near Causeway Bay, you can pay rent-a-curse grannies to punch your enemy. For HK$50 these curse-muttering sorceresses will use a shoe to pound the hell out of a paper cut-out of anyone vexing you. Villain exorcism (打小人, *da siu yan*) is believed to bring resolution to real-world problems.

⑥ Vegetarian in a Market

Gun Gei (根記健康素食; ☑852 2575 7595; No 6 Bowrington Rd Market & Cooked Food Centre, 21 Bowrington Rd, Wan Chai; dishes HK$32-70; ⏰8.30am-2.30pm & 5.30-9.30pm Mon-Sat; ☑; Ⓜ Causeway Bay, exit A) inside the Bowrington Road Market makes simple and tasty vegetarian dishes. If going for dinner, it's best to have a Chinese-speaker help you book a table and pre-order dishes – the place is often packed.

A **B** **C** **D**

0 500 m
0 0.25 miles

1

2

Lung Wui Rd

Lung Wui Rd

Tim Wa Ave

Tim Mei Ave

Fenwick Pier St

Hong Kong Convention & Exhibition Centre

Expo Dr

Convention Ave
Hong Kong Convention & Exhibition Centre

WAN CHAI

4
Tamar Park

24

Harcourt Rd

Lambeth St

Drake St

Tamar

Cotton Tree Dr

Admiralty Ⓜ

Harcourt Garden

ADMIRALTY

Queensway

Arsenal St

Jaffe Rd

Lockhart Rd

Fenwick St

Luard Rd

O'Brien Rd

Gloucester R

14
Hong Kong Park

Pacific Place

Justice Dr

Hennessy Rd

Anton St

Queen's Rd East

Southorn Playground

30

Ⓜ Wan Chai

Thoms Rd

Johnston Rd

3

4

Kennedy Rd

Borrett Rd

6 Asia Society Hong Kong Centre

Star St

22
26

Swatow St

Ship St

16

Lee Tung St

20

29

Cross St

Wan Chai

2
Hung Shing Temple

Bowen Dr

Blu Hou

21

18

Bowen Rd

Bowen Rd

Lung On St
Stone Nullah La

1
Pak Ta Temple

5

For reviews see	
◉ Top Sights	p62
◉ Sights	p70
✖ Eating	p72
🍷 Drinking	p74
★ Entertainment	p77
🔒 Shopping	p78

E   F   G   H

1

2

3

4

5

VICTORIA HARBOUR

Causeway Bay Typhoon Shelter

Causeway Bay

Kellett Island

Cargo Handling Basin

Hung Hing Rd

Wan Chai Sports Ground

Tonnochy Rd

Marsh Rd

CAUSEWAY BAY

Cannon St

Houston St

🚇 19

Victoria Park

7

Gloucester Rd

Harbour Rd

Jaffe Rd

Percival St

Paterson St

31

Harbour Dr

Stewart Rd

Jaffe Rd

Lockhart Rd

Marsh Rd

Canal Rd

Causeway Bay

8

Lockhart Rd

Great George St

M

28

Kai Chiu Rd

Yee Wo St

23

12

17

Russell St

27

Lee Garden Rd

Yun Ping Rd

Pennington St

Haven St

10

Hennessy Rd

13

Wan Chai Rd

Bowrington Rd

Yat Sin St

Matheson St

9

Hysan Ave

32

25

11

5

Comix Home Base

Cross La

Wood Rd

Heard St

MORRISON HILL

Oi Kwan Rd

Yiu Wa St

Leighton Rd

Leighton Rd

CAROLINE HILL

Caroline Hill Rd

Broadwood Link Rd

Wan Chai Park

Queen's Rd East

SportsRd

Wong Nai Chung Rd

LEIGHTON HILL

Stubbs Rd

Hau Tak La

Wong Nai Chung Rd

Happy Valley Racecourse

Ventris Rd

HAPPY VALLEY

Sights

Pak Tai Temple

TAOIST TEMPLE

1 ◉ Map p68, D5

A short stroll up Stone Nullah Lane takes you to a majestic Taoist temple built in 1863 to honour a god of the sea, Pak Tai. The temple, the largest on Hong Kong Island, is impressive. The ceramic roof ridge ornaments depicting scenes from Cantonese opera were made in Shiwan – a beautiful example of Lingnan architecture in Hong Kong. The main hall of the temple has a formidable 3m-tall copper likeness of Pak Tai cast during the Ming dynasty. (北帝廟; 2 Lung On St, Wan Chai; ⏰8am-5pm; Ⓜ Wan Chai, exit A3)

Hung Shing Temple

BUDDHIST TEMPLE

2 ◉ Map p68, C4

Nestled in a nook on the southern side of Queen's Rd East, this dark and rather forbidding temple is built atop huge boulders that used to overlook the harbour. It was erected around 1850 in honour of a deified Tang-dynasty official known for his virtue (important) and ability to make predictions of value to traders (ultra-important). (洪聖古廟; 129-131 Queen's Rd E, Wan Chai; ⏰8.30am-5.30pm; 🚌6, 6A, Ⓜ Wan Chai, exit A3)

Blue House

ARCHITECTURE

3 ◉ Map p68, D5

The Blue House, built in the 1920s, and its neighbours **Yellow House** (黃屋; 📞852 2835 4376; http://houseofstories.sjs.org.hk; 2-8 Hing Wan St, Wan Chai; 🚌6, 6A) and **Orange House** (橙屋; 📞852 2835 4376; http://houseofstories.sjs.org.hk; 8 King Sing St, Wan Chai; 🚌6, 6A), make up a heritage cluster known as 'Viva Blue House' (We 嘩藍屋). The star of the lot, Blue House is a graceful four-storey tenement building featuring cast-iron Spanish balconies reminiscent of New Orleans. It is being restored and will reopen around mid-2017 with a dessert shop, a renovated osteopathy clinic, and toilets for its dozen residents. During its closure, **House of Stories** (香港故事館; 📞852 2835 4376; http://houseofstories.sjs.org.hk; 74 Stone Nullah Lane, Wan Chai; ⏰11am-6pm Thu-Tue; 🚌6, 6A) will relocate to Yellow House. (藍屋; 📞852 2835 4376; http://houseofstories.sjs.org.hk; 72-74A Stone Nullah Lane, Wan Chai; 🚌6, 6A)

Tamar Park

PARK

4 ◉ Map p68, B2

This harbour-front park on the site of the New Central Government Offices (新政府總部) is an inviting sprawl of verdant lawns where you can sunbathe while watching the ships go by. It's part of a 4km promenade along the northern shoreline of Hong Kong Island, from Central Piers, outside the IFC mall, past Wan Chai, all the way to North Point. Concerts and art events take place here occasionally, as did the major protest known as the Umbrella Movement in 2014. (添馬公園; Harcourt Rd, Admiralty; Ⓜ Admiralty, exit A)

Hung Shing Temple

Comix Home Base   MUSEUM

5 Map p68, E4

Housed in 10 historic buildings from the 1910s, this airy museum shines a spotlight on Hong Kong's talented comic-book artists, including a few international-award winners. A library, exhibitions, video footage and workshops introduce visitors to the city's rich comic-book history, from classics depicting wartime struggles *(Renjian Pictorial)* and satires on life in a British colony *(Old Master Q)*, through Ma Wing-shing's martial-arts comics, to the pensive creations of younger artists such as Chi Hoi. (☎852 2824 5303; www.comixhomebase. hk; 7 Mallory St, Wan Chai; admission free; ⊗10am-8pm; Ⓜ Wan Chai, exit A3)

Asia Society Hong Kong Centre   HISTORIC BUILDING

6 Map p68, B4

An architectural feat, this magnificent site integrates 19th-century British military buildings, including a couple of explosives magazines, and transforms them into an exhibition gallery, a multipurpose theatre, an excellent restaurant and a bookshop, all open to the public. The architects Tod Williams and Billie Tsien eschewed bold statements for a subdued design that deferred to history and the natural shape of the land. The result is a horizontally oriented site that offers an uplifting contrast to the skyscrapers nearby. Experience it with a meal at **AMMO** (☎852 2537 9888; www.ammo.com.hk; mains HK$118-400;

⊙noon-midnight Sun-Thu, to 1am Fri & Sat). (亞洲協會香港中心, Hong Kong Jockey Club Former Explosives Magazine; ☑852 2103 9511; www.asiasociety.org/hong-kong; 9 Justice Dr, Admiralty; ⊙gallery 11am-5pm Tue-Sun, to 7pm last Thu of month; Ⓜ Admiralty, exit F)

Victoria Park PARK

7 ⊙ Map p68, H2

Built on land reclaimed from the **Causeway Bay Typhoon Shelter** (銅鑼灣避風塘; off Hung Hing Rd, Causeway Bay; Ⓜ Causeway Bay, exit D1), Victoria Park is the biggest patch of public greenery on Hong Kong Island. The best time to go is on a weekday morning, when it becomes a forest of people practising the slow-motion choreography of taichi. The park becomes a flower market just before the Lunar New Year and a lantern museum during the **Mid-Autumn Festival**. The swimming pool (previously outdoor), built in 1957, was Hong Kong's oldest. (維多利亞公園; www.lcsd.gov.hk/en/ls_park.php; Causeway Rd, Causeway Bay; admission free; ⊙park 24hr; ⛹; Ⓜ Tin Hau, exit B)

Eating

Atum Desserant SWEETS $

8 ✕ Map p68, G3

Hop onto a stool, hook your bag under the counter and watch museum-worthy desserts materialise with some help from liquid nitrogen and the owner's years as a pastry chef at the Mandarin Oriental. Improvisation

(HK$348 for two) is confectionery, fruits and ice-cream arranged like a Jackson Pollock crossbred with a Monet. And it's not just for show – flavours are surprisingly well balanced. (☑852 2956 1411, 852 2377 2400; www.atumhk.com; 16th fl, The L Square, 459-461 Lockhart Rd, Causeway Bay; desserts from HK$138; ⊙2.45pm-midnight Mon-Thu, from 1pm Fri-Sun; Ⓜ Causeway Bay, exit C)

Fortune Kitchen CANTONESE $$

9 ✕ Map p68, G3

Despite the old-fashioned Chinatown name, Fortune Kitchen is decorated like an old tea house and serves homey but sophisticated Cantonese at wallet-friendly prices. The owner was a sous-chef at a Michelin-star restaurant and his culinary skills are evident in dishes such as the signature steamed chicken with dried scallops and the eponymous fried rice. Booking advised. (盈福小廚; ☑852 2697 7317; 5 Lan Fong Rd, Causeway Bay; mains HK$100-500; ⊙11.30am-5pm & 6-10.30pm; Ⓜ Causeway Bay, exit A)

Joy Hing Roasted Meat CANTONESE $

10 ✕ Map p68, E3

This basic stall is one of your best bets for Cantonese barbecue (the Michelin inspectors think so too) – succulent slivers of barbecued pork, goose, chicken and liver over freshly steamed rice. The menu is simply cards stuck on the wall. Just see what your neighbours are having and point. (再興燒臘飯店; ☑852 2519 6639; 1C Stewart Rd, Wan Chai;

meals HK$30-60; ⏱10am-10pm; Ⓜ Wan Chai, exit A4)

Kam's Roast Goose CANTONESE $

11 🍴 Map p68, E4

One of two spin-offs from Central's famed **Yung Kee Restaurant** (鏞記; ☎852 2522 1624; www.yungkee.com. hk; 32-40 Wellington St, Lan Kwai Fong; lunch HK$150-400, dinner from HK$450; ⏱11am-10.30pm; 🐾; Ⓜ Central, exit D2), Kam's clearly still upholds the same strict standards in the sourcing and roasting of the city's most glorified roast goose. Besides the juicy crisp-skinned fowl (of which the best cut is the leg), other barbecued meats such as roast suckling pig are well worth sinking your teeth into. (甘牌燒鵝; ☎852 2520 1110; www.krg.com.hk; 226 Hennessy Rd, Wan Chai; meals HK$70-200; ⏱11.30am-9pm; Ⓜ Wan Chai, exit A2)

Seventh Son CANTONESE $$

12 🍴 Map p68, F3

Worthy spin-off from the illustrious **Fook Lam Moon** (福臨門; ☎852 2366 0286; www.fooklammoon-grp.com; Shop 8, 1st fl, 53-59 Kimberley Rd, Tsim Sha Tsui; meals HK$400-2000; ⏱11.30am-2.30pm & 6-10.30pm; Ⓜ Tsim Sha Tsui, exit B1) (aka Tycoon's Canteen), Seventh Son reproduces to a tee FLM's homestyle dishes and a few extravagant seafood numbers as well. The food here is excellent, plus you get the treatment FLM reserves for regulars. Moot point, though – you wouldn't know how regulars are treated at FLM unless you are one. (家全七福; ☎852 2892 2888; www.seventhson.hk; 5 & 6th fl, Kwan Chart Tower, 6 Tonnochy Rd, Wan Chai; meals from HK$350; ⏱11.30am-3pm & 6-10.30pm; Ⓜ Wan Chai, exit C)

Kin's Kitchen

CANTONESE $$

13 Map p68, F3

Art critic-turned-restaurateur Lau Kin-wai infuses his artistic sense and passion for local ingredients into this understated restaurant specialising in Cantonese classics with a twist. Lau, looking quite the *bon vivant* with silver hair and rosy cheeks, is sometimes seen discussing the merits of the four kinds of white rice on the menu with customers. (留家廚房; ☏852 2571 0913; 5th fl, W Square, 314-324 Hennessy Rd, Wan Chai; meals HK$180-450; ⊙noon-3pm & 6-11pm; Ⓜ Wan Chai, exit A2)

Lock Cha Tea Shop

VEGETARIAN, CHINESE $

14 Map p68, A3

Set in the lush environs of Hong Kong Park, Lock Cha offers fragrant teas and tasty vegetarian dim sum in a replica of an ancient scholar's study. It also hosts Chinese music performances on Saturday (7pm to 9pm) and Sunday (4pm to 6pm). Do call to reserve a seat. The music is popular; the tea shop is dainty. (樂茶軒; ☏852

Top Tip
Green Dining
When having seafood, avoid eating deepwater fish and shark's fin. The World Wildlife Fund (WWF) has a sustainable seafood guide you can download (www.wwf.org.hk)

2801 7177; www.lockcha.com; Ground fl, KS Lo Gallery, 10 Cotton Tree Dr, Hong Kong Park, Admiralty; dim sum HK$15-28, tea from HK$25; ⊙10am-8pm, closed second Tue; 🖉; Ⓜ Admiralty, exit C1)

Serge et le Phoque

MODERN FRENCH $$$

15 Map p68, D4

Expect to see wet-market butchers chopping meat through the floor-to-ceiling windows (it's harder for them to look in) as you savour the perfect French beef or giant Japanese scallops in casual cool-toned luxury, pondering which side of the gentrification debate you're on. The restaurant, open only for dinner, is dimly lit by milk-white orbs from the '60s. (☏852 5465 2000; Shop B2, ground fl, Tower 1, The Zenith, 3 Wan Chai Rd, Wan Chai; dinner set from HK$700; ⊙6-10.30pm; Ⓜ Wan Chai, exit A3)

Drinking

Botanicals

BAR

16 Map p68, C4

Botanicals draws after-work imbibers with real vegetation, chic furnishings in a green-compatible palette, craft beer, inventive cocktails flavoured with herbs from its rooftop farm, and reinvented pub food. Opening hours may change, so call before going to be safe. (☏852 2866 3444; www.thepawn.com.hk; 62 Johnston Rd, Wan Chai; ⊙4pm-12.30am; Ⓜ Wan Chai, exit A3)

Famous crispy goose delicacy at Kam's Roast Goose (p73)

Cafe Corridor CAFE

17 🍷 Map p68, G3

Tucked away in the back of a narrow corridor, this nifty 15-year-old cafe with a dozen seats offers handcrafted Yirgacheffe coffee and all-day breakfast to regulars or anyone seeking respite from the Times Square drama across the street. Dim lighting and a feature wall keep it cosy. And people come to chat – the cafe has no wi-fi. (🖀852 2892 2927; 26A Russell St, Causeway Bay; ⏰8am-10pm Mon-Thu, to 11pm Fri, 10am-11pm Sat & Sun; Ⓜ Causeway Bay, exit A)

Tai Lung Fung BAR

18 🍷 Map p68, D5

This capriciously retro bar takes its name from a 1960s Cantonese opera troupe. In common parlance, Tai Lung Fung (Big Dragon Phoenix) means 'much ado'. Appropriately the decor is fabulously over-the-top. Tai Lung Fung attracts artsy types who prefer its funky aesthetics and quiet environment to a more conventional partying vibe. Cocktails, less adventurous than the decor, are the speciality. (大龍鳳; 🖀852 2572 0055; 5-9 Hing Wan St, Wan Chai; ⏰noon-1am Mon-Thu, to 1.30am Fri & Sat, happy hour noon-9pm; Ⓜ Wan Chai, exit A3)

International Dragon Boat Race (p78)

Elephant Grounds

CAFE

19 Map p68, H2

With a chilled-out ambience, young upbeat staff, spot-on coffee, and branches in Sheung Wan and Aberdeen, Elephant Grounds is easily Hong Kong's hottest new coffee hang-out. The popularity of its brews is surpassed only by that of its chunky ice-cream sandwiches. Its food menu is also fancier than most cafe chow – eggs Benedict comes in a taco for instance. (☏852 2253 1313; www.elephantgrounds.com; Shop C, 42-48 Paterson St, Fashion Walk, Causeway Bay; Ⓜ Causeway Bay, exit D2)

MyHouse

WINE BAR

20 Map p68, D4

MyHouse brings together vinyls and natural wine in a spacious Euro-chic setting. Furniture is made from natural wood, illuminated wine bottles hang alongside cured meats, and guests can take their pick from a vinyl library, slip it on individual turntables, and kick back with an organic, chemical-free Beaujolais, or surrender to the whims of a resident DJ (analogue, of course). (☏852 2323 1715; www.myhousehk.com; 26th fl, QRE Plaza, 202 Queen's Rd E, Wan Chai; ◷6pm-2am Tue & Wed, to 3am Thu-Sat, closed Sun; Ⓜ Wan Chai, exit A3)

Stone Nullah Tavern BAR

21 Map p68, D5

A fancified American 'farmhouse' tavern that stocks an impressive range of American whiskeys and bourbons, bottles from Francis Ford Coppola's vineyard, and Californian ale – all to be enjoyed amid white-tiled walls, vintage wine cabinets and a mule-deer taxidermy mount. French windows capitalise on the bar's location in a scenic and historic part of Wan Chai. (852 3182 0128; www.stonenullahtavern.com; 69 Stone Nullah Lane, Wan Chai; noon-1am; Wan Chai, exit A3)

Ted's Lookout BAR

22 Map p68, C4

Ted's is hip. The concrete facade features theatre tip-up seats and the bar's name in marquee lights, while white-tiled walls and gas lanterns decorate the interior. It's also laid-back – neighbours like to nurse a beer here in easy clothes, especially during the day. The burgers are good too, but you can smell them being fried in the open kitchen. (852 5533 9369; Moonful Court, 17A Moon St, Wan Chai; 5-11pm Mon-Fri, noon-11pm Sat & Sun; Admiralty, exit F)

Entertainment

Focal Fair LIVE MUSIC

23 Map p68, H3

Finally a conveniently located indie music venue – Focal Fair is right by the Hong Kong Central Library! It hosts several gigs a month, and everyone from Canadian hardcore punks Career Suicide to local noise artists Dennis Wong and Eric Chan have played here. See the Facebook page for the latest. (www.facebook.com/focal-fair; 28th fl, Park Avenue Tower, 5 Moreton Terrace, Causeway Bay; Tin Hau, exit A1)

Local Life

The **Street Music Concert Series** (街頭音樂系列; http://hkstreetmusic.com) refers to the wonderful outdoor concerts thrown by eclectic musician Kung Chi-shing, that have captivated consul generals and street sleepers with their balance of tight curation and fizzy spontaneity. Genres range from indie rock to Cantonese opera, Bluegrass to Bach. You're bound to find something you like, even if it's just the atmosphere.

Concerts happen monthly at the Arts Centre (p78) from 5.30pm to 8pm on the third Saturday of the month, at Comix Home Base (p71) from 3pm to 4.30pm every fourth Sunday, and at Blue House (p70) from 7.30pm to 9pm on the second Thursday of the month, with occasional events in other parts of town. The website has more details.

Hong Kong Arts Centre

DANCE, THEATRE

24 Map p68, C3

A popular venue for dance, theatre and music performances, the Arts Centre has theatres, a cinema and a gallery. (香港藝術中心; ☎852 2582 0200; www.hkac.org.hk; 2 Harbour Rd, Wan Chai; Ⓜ Wan Chai, exit C)

Shopping

Hola Classic

CLOTHING

25 🔒 Map p68, H4

This nifty little shop is known for its highly affordable made-to-measure suits, jackets and shirts for men. Don't expect impeccable fabrics (they don't dress the British monarchy), but a two-piece suit starts from only HK$2280. Hola can even make Oxfords, with purple tassels too if that's how you

---

Understand
Hong Kong Festivals

Hong Kong's calendar is full of traditional Chinese and Western festivals, as well as those promoting the arts and sports. Here are some of the best:

Hong Kong Arts Festival (香港藝術節; www.hk.artsfestival.org; from HK$150; ⏲ Feb-Mar) An extravaganza of music, drama and dance, featuring some of the world's top performers.

Hong Kong Sevens (www.hksevens.com.hk; ⏲ late Mar or early Apr) Rugby teams from all over the world come for three days of lightning-fast, 15-minute matches.

Hong Kong International Film Festival (香港國際電影節; www.hkiff.org.hk; from HK$45; ⏲ Mar & Apr) Asia's top film festival.

Art Basel Hong Kong (香港巴塞爾藝術展; www.artbasel.com/hong-kong; HK$180-850; ⏲ Mar) Local and international galleries participate in Asia's premier art fair.

International Dragon Boat Race (香港國際龍舟邀請賽; www.hkdba.com.hk; ⏲ May or Jun) Hundreds of teams from all around the world compete in Victoria Harbour.

Hong Kong Photo Festival (香港國際攝影節; www.hkphotofest.org) A biennial event that highlights the works of Hong Kong's photographers. See the website for dates.

Clockenflap Outdoor Music Festival (香港音樂及藝術節; www.clockenflap.com; tickets HK$600-1800; ⏲ Nov or Dec) This outdoor indie event in November is the highlight of Hong Kong's live-music calendar.

roll. The shoe shop is 30 seconds away at 13A Haven St. (📞852 2870 0246; 11A Caroline Hill Rd, Causeway Bay; 🕐12.30-9pm; Ⓜ Causeway Bay, exit A)

Kapok FASHION & ACCESSORIES

26 🔒 Map p68, C4

In the hip Star St area, this boutique has a fastidiously edited selection of luxe-cool local and international clothing and accessory labels. Look for the Kapok-label made-in-HK men's shirts, and graphic Mischa handbags by local designer Michelle Lai. A sister boutique is around the corner at 3 Sun St. It also has a corner at Eslite (p79) bookstore. (📞852 2549 9254; www.ka-pok.com; 5 St Francis Yard, Wan Chai; 🕐11am-8pm, to 6pm Sun; Ⓜ Admiralty, exit F)

Yiu Fung Store FOOD

27 🔒 Map p68, G3

Hong Kong's most famous store (c 1960s) for Chinese pickles and preserved fruit features sour plum, liquorice-flavoured lemon, tangerine peel, pickled papaya and dried longan. Just before the Lunar New Year, it's crammed with shoppers. (么鳳; 📞852 2576 2528; Shop A, 2 Pak Sha Rd, Causeway Bay; 🕐11am-10.30pm; Ⓜ Causeway Bay, exit A)

Eslite BOOKS

28 🔒 Map p68, G3

You could spend an entire evening inside this swanky three-floor Taiwanese bookstore, which features a massive

collection of English and Chinese books and magazines, a shop selling gorgeous stationery and leather-bound journals, a cafe, a bubble-tea counter, and a huge kids' toy and book section. (誠品; 📞852 3419 6789; 8th-10th fl, Hysan Place, 500 Hennessy Rd, Causeway Bay; 🕐10am-10pm Sun-Thu, to 11pm Fri & Sat; 👶; Ⓜ Causeway Bay, exit F2)

Tai Yuen Street Toy Shops TOYS

29 🔒 Map p68, D4

Tai Yuen St is known as 'toy street' thanks to a handful of shops that carry every toy, game and knick-knack your child could ever want – not to mention party gear. The quality is no better than Toys R Us, but prices are cheaper and choices are overwhelming. A couple of these shops stock vintage mechanical tin collectibles behind glass. Bring a shopping bag. (太原街玩具店; 14-19 Tai Yuen St, Wan Chai; 🕐10am-7.30pm; Ⓜ Wan Chai, exit A3)

Clockenflap Outdoor Music Festival (p78)

Wan Chai Computer Centre
ELECTRONICS

30 Map p68, D4

This gleaming, beeping warren of tiny shops is a safe bet for anything digital and electronic. (灣仔電腦城; 1st fl, Southorn Centre, 130-138 Hennessy Rd, Wan Chai; ⏰10am-9pm Mon-Sat, noon-8pm Sun; MWan Chai, exit B2)

Fashion Walk
CLOTHING

31 Map p69, H3

A mostly street-level fashion-shopping mecca spanning four streets in Causeway Bay – Paterson, Cleveland, Great George and Kingston. It's where you'll find big names like Paul Smith, Comme des Garcons and Kiehl's, but also up-and-coming local brands, and shops with off-the-rack high-street labels. (www.fashionwalk.com.hk; ⏰office 10am-11pm; MCauseway Bay, D4)

Numb Workshop
CLOTHING

32 Map p69, H4

A stark minimalist shop that stocks androgynous monochrome garments that will hide your love handles or have you looking like a stylish ninja, depending on the style and your shape. We particularly liked the details on the black twill zip trousers. (☎852 2312 7007; www.numbworkshop. com; 25 Haven St, Causeway Bay; ⏰1-10pm; MCauseway Bay, exit A)

Understand
Pollution in Hong Kong

Air Quality

Hong Kong's most pressing environmental problem is air pollution, responsible for more than 2000 premature deaths a year. Not surprisingly, it has become a highly charged political and economic issue. Mounting public pressure has forced the government to take more decisive measures in recent years to control emissions from vehicles and power plants, the major source of air pollution. Government statistics show that the emission of most air pollutants has gone down. That said, many travellers to Hong Kong might find it hard to breathe in congested areas such as Causeway Bay and Mong Kok, where air quality often exceeds the safe limit set by the World Health Organisation (WHO).

The Hong Kong government's Air Quality Health Index (AQHI) monitors Hong Kong's air quality and alerts the public to potential health risks posed by excessive exposure to air pollutants through a website (www.aqhi.gov.hk/tc.html) and mobile application.

Waste

Three large landfills in the New Territories absorb all of Hong Kong's daily 15,000 tonnes of municipal waste (though they will soon be full). As space for building large landfills is limited, the government introduced waste reduction schemes in 1998, but progress has been slow. Only 37% of solid waste is recycled.

Looking Ahead

The future of Hong Kong's environment will depend not only on the city's efforts, but also on whether pollution in the greater Pearl River Delta region is tamed. The most polluted water in Hong Kong is found in Deep Bay, which is shared with nearby Shēnzhèn, and Hong Kong's air quality deteriorates drastically when winds bring pollution from the north. The governments of Hong Kong and Guǎngdōng are working together to tackle regional pollution. Progress has been slow, and rising tension between Hong Kong and mainland China is an obstacle to future collaboration.

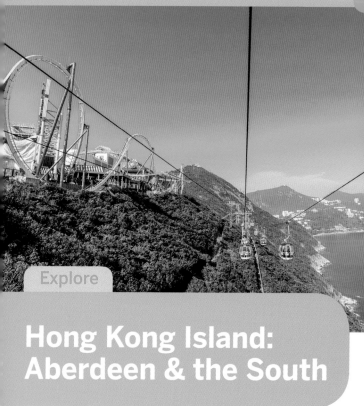

Explore

Hong Kong Island: Aberdeen & the South

This is Hong Kong Island's backyard playground – from the beaches of Repulse Bay, Deep Water Bay and South Bay to shoppers' paradise Stanley Market and Horizon Plaza, and the excellent Ocean Park amusement park near Aberdeen.

The Sights in a Day

 Take the bus to Stanley. Explore the village and comb its **market** (p85) for gifts. Go on a tour of the historic **St Stephen's College** (p85), if you've reserved in advance. Have lunch at **Smugglers Inn** (p91).

 Make your way to Pok Fu Lam. Tour the gorgeous **Bethanie** (p88) and check out the old dairy farm sites in **Pok Fu Lam Village** (p89) and the vicinity. Head south to the famous Aberdeen Typhoon Shelter. Take in the smells of the harbour and of drying fish along the **promenade** (p87), and embark on the half-hour sampan tour (p88).

If there's time, shop for designer bargains at **Horizon Plaza** (p93) in Ap Lei Chau on the other side of the typhoon shelter. Then feast on cheap and tasty seafood at the **Ap Lei Chau Market Cooked Food Centre** (p90).

For a local's day in Aberdeen and the South, see p84.

Local Life

Beach-Hopping on Island South (p84)

Best of Hong Kong

Sights
Young Master Ales (p88)

Eating
Aberdeen Fish Market Yee Hope Seafood Restaurant (p89)

Ap Lei Chau Market Cooked Food Centre (p90)

Verandah (p85)

Getting There

Bus Stanley, Repulse Bay & Deep Water Bay: buses 6A, 6X, 260 from below Exchange Sq (Central); 73, 973 from Aberdeen.

Bus Aberdeen: buses 73 and 973 from Stanley.

Bus Ap Lei Chau: bus 90 from Admiralty bus terminus; by commuter boat from Aberdeen Promenade.

Local Life
Beach-Hopping on Island South

Beach-hopping along the Island's southern coastline is fun and convenient. Lots of beaches have showers, and most have other sights and restaurants in the vicinity. In the summer the waters around Stanley and Repulse Bay teem with bioluminescent algae. Go after sundown to feel like you're swimming with fireflies.

1 Deep Water Bay

Start from the westernmost **Deep Water Bay** (深水灣; 🚌 6, 6A, 6X, 260), a quiet little inlet with a beach flanked by shade trees. Though not as famous as its neighbour Repulse Bay, it's less crowded and its barbecue pits are a real draw for locals – a dip here, especially in late afternoon, is sometimes accompanied by the tantalising aromas of grilled meat.

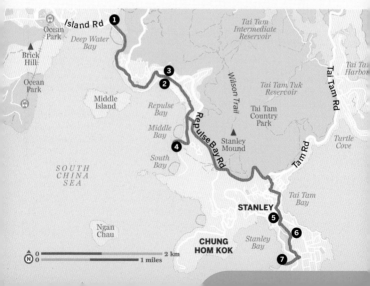

❷ Repulse Bay

From Deep Water Bay, walk 2km via the scenic Seaview Promenade to **Repulse Bay** (淺水灣; 🚌6, 6A, 6X, 260). The long beach with tawny sand and murky water is packed almost all the time in summer. At its southeast end there's an assembly of deities and figures, all expressed in garish cartoon kitsch. The hills here are strewn with luxury residences, including a wavy pastel building with a square hole, a feature related to feng shui.

❸ Verandah Restaurant

The elegant **Verandah** (露台餐廳; 📞852 2292 2822; www.therepulsebay.com; 1st fl, 109 Repulse Bay Rd, Repulse Bay; meals from HK$600; ⏰noon-2.30pm, 3-5.30pm & 7-10.30pm daily, brunch 11am-2.30pm Sun; 🚌6, 6A, 6X, 260) drips with colonial nostalgia, with its grand piano, marble staircase and wooden ceiling fans. The afternoon tea is the best this side of Hong Kong Island. Book ahead.

❹ Middle & South Bay

These attractive beaches are 1km and 2km to the south of Repulse Bay respectively. Middle Bay is popular with gay beach goers, while French expats are drawn to South Bay. Swimming here on summer nights, you'll see specks of algae glowing like stars in the water.

❺ St Stephen's Beach

This hidden **bolt-hole** (聖士提反灣泳灘; 🚌6A, 14) south of Stanley village is cleaner than Stanley Main Beach, and there are windsurfing boards and kayaks for hire. Take the bus to Stanley then walk south along Wong Ma Kok Rd. Turn right into Wong Ma Kok Path, then turn south and go past the boathouse to the beach.

❻ Stanley Market

No big bargains or big stings at this **market** (赤柱市集; Stanley Village Rd, Stanley; ⏰9am-6pm; 🚌6, 6A, 6X or 260), just reasonably priced casual clothes (including big sizes and children's wear), bric-a-brac, souvenirs and formulaic art, all in a nicely confusing maze of alleys running down to Stanley Bay. Do bargain here, but not aggressively. It's best to go during the week when the market isn't bursting with tourists and locals.

❼ St Stephen's College

WWII history buffs should visit the beautiful and historic campus of **St Stephen's College** (聖士提反書院文物徑; 📞852 2813 0360; www.ssc.edu.hk/ssctrail/eng; 22 Tung Tau Wan Rd, Stanley; admission free; 🚌6, 6A, 6X, 260), which sits next to Stanley Military Cemetery, southeast of Stanley Market. Founded in 1903, the school was turned into an emergency military hospital on the eve of the Japanese invasion of Hong Kong in 1941 and became an internment camp after the city fell. Admission to the trail is by a two-hour guided tour only – reserve in advance via the website.

SIU
SAI
WAN

CHAI
WAN

Tai Tam Rd

Pottinger
Peak
(312m)

Big Wave Bay Rd

Hong Kong Trail

Shek O
Country
Park

SHEK O
8
13

Shek O Rd

Shek O Peak
(284m)

Shek O Beach

D'Aguilar
Peak
(323m)

SOUTH
CHINA
SEA

Tai Tam Harbour

Tai Tam Rd

Tai Tam
Country
Park

Tai Tam
Reservoir

Tai Tam
Country
Park

Tai Tam Tuk
Reservoir

Tai Tam Rd

Stanley
Mound
(386m)

STANLEY
15 12
14

Stanley
Bay

Hong Kong Trail

Mt Butler
(436m)

Jardine's
Lookout ▲

Stubbs Rd

Mt Nicholson
(430m)

Violet Hill
(433m)

Tai Tam
Intermediate
Reservoir

Wilson Trail

Repulse Bay Rd

CHUNG
HOM
KOK

Repulse
Bay

South
Bay

Middle
Island

Ngan
Chau

THE
PEAK

Pok Fu Lam
Village
7

Béthanie
3

Aberdeen
Country
Park

Aberdeen
Lower
Reservoir

Hong Kong Trail

Blindspot
Gallery

Aberdeen
Country
Park

ABERDEEN
9 1
5
11

Aberdeen
Promenade

Hung Shing
Temple

AP LEI
CHAU
16 4

10

Ocean
Park
2

Deep
Water
Bay

Brick
Hill

WONG
CHUK
HANG
6

Ocean
Park

Sham
Wan

Aberdeen
Channel

Ap Lei
Pai

Young
Master
Ales

East Lamma Channel

MO TAT
WAN

Lamma

N

For reviews see
⊙ Sights   p87
✕ Eating   p89
● Drinking   p91
🛍 Shopping   p93

0   2 miles
0   4 km

SEAONWEB/GETTY IMAGES ©

Aberdeen Promenade

Sights

Aberdeen Promenade WATERFRONT

1  Map p86, A2

Tree-lined Aberdeen Promenade runs from west to east on Aberdeen Praya Rd across the water from Ap Lei Chau. On its western end is sprawling **Aberdeen Wholesale Fish Market** (香港仔魚市場; Aberdeen Promenade, Aberdeen) with its industrial-strength water tanks teeming with marine life. It's pungent and grimy, but 100% Hong Kong. Before reaching the market, you'll pass berthed house boats and seafood-processing vessels. (We detected a karaoke parlour or two as well.) (香港仔海濱公園; Aberdeen Praya Rd, Aberdeen; admission free)

Ocean Park AMUSEMENT PARK

2  Map p86, B2

Despite the crowd-pulling powers of Disneyland on Lantau, for many Ocean Park remains the most popular theme park in Hong Kong. Constant expansion, new rides and thrills, and the presence of four giant pandas and two rare red pandas ensure the park remains a huge draw for families. Be aware that in part of the park, Marine World, cetaceans are kept in captivity and there are performances involving dolphins and orcas, which scientific studies suggest are harmful to these animals. (海洋公園; ☎852 3923 2323; www.oceanpark.com.hk; Ocean Park Rd; adult/child 3-11yr HK$385/193; ⏱10am-7.30pm; ♿; ☒629 from Admiralty, ☒973 from Tsim Sha

Tsui, 6A, 6X, 70, 75 from Central, 72, 72A, 92 from Causeway Bay)

Béthanie   HISTORIC BUILDING

3 Map p86, A1

Perched on hilly Pok Fu Lam, a college and residential area northwest of Aberdeen, this beautiful restoration is a highlight in this part of town.

 Local Life

Sampan Tours

Sampan tours are a great way to see parts of the island's south coast. You can find sampan operators milling around the eastern end of the Aberdeen Promenade. Usually they charge HK$50 to HK$80 per person for a 30-minute ride, around HK$130 to Sok Kwu Wan and HK$160 to Yung Shue Wan on Lamma.

If you want just a glimpse of the harbour, you can take the small ferry across to Ap Lei Chau Island (adult/child under 12 HK$2.20/1.20) between 6am and midnight. Alternatively, just hop on the free ferry to **Jumbo Kingdom Floating Restaurant** (珍寶海鮮舫; ☏852 2553 9111; www.jumbo.com.hk; Shum Wan Pier Dr, Wong Chuk Hang; meals from HK$200; ☉11am-11.30pm Mon-Sat, from 9am Sun; ☐90 from Central) and come back.

The promenade is easily accessed from Aberdeen bus terminus via a pedestrian subway under Aberdeen Praya Rd.

The complex, which now houses a film school, was built by the French Mission in 1875 as a sanatorium for priests from all over Asia to rest and recover from tropical diseases before they returned to their missions. (伯大尼; ☏852 2854 8918; www.hkapa.edu/asp/general/general_visitors.asp; 139 Pok Fu Lam Rd, Pok Fu Lam; HK$33; ☉11am-6pm Mon-Sat, from noon Sun; ☐7, 40, 40M, 90B, 91)

Young Master Ales   BREWERY

4 Map p86, A2

You can visit Hong Kong's own craft brewery most Saturday afternoons, but email ahead to inform them you're coming. It's possible to arrange a tasting tour on other days. YMA offers a selection of non-filtered, chemical-free ales that range from crisp to robust. We enjoyed the limited edition Mood for Spring with its floral infusions. (少爺麥啤; www.youngmasterales.com; Units 407-9, Oceanic Industrial Centre, 2 Lee Lok St, Ap Lei Chau; ☉noon-5pm Sat, or by appointment; ☐671, 90B)

Hung Shing Temple   TAOIST TEMPLE

5 Map p86, B2

Renovated many times since it was built in 1773 by local fishermen, Ap Lei Chau's major temple is dedicated to Hung Shing, the protector of seafarers. Its major features are a sea-facing orientation (which is believed to bring good feng shui), the fine Shiwan figurines on the roof ridges (which denote its significance), and the two timber 'dragon poles' in its forecourt, which are said to counter the 'death-like aura' of the **Aberdeen Police Station** (舊香港仔警署; ☎852 2873 2244; 116 Aberdeen Main Rd, Aberdeen; ☉10am-10pm Tue, Thu & Fri, to 6pm Mon, Wed & Sat; ⊞27) across the water. (洪聖古廟; Hung Shing St, Ap Lei Chau; ☉8am-5pm; ⊞Ap Lei Chau)

Blindspot Gallery GALLERY

6 ◉ Map p86, B2

So named because the owner believed that contemporary photography was not getting the attention it deserved in Hong Kong, Blindspot Gallery features the works of photographers and artists from Hong Kong and Asia, including Stanley Wong, Ken Kitano and Maleonn. Arguably one of the best places to acquaint yourself with Hong Kong and Asian photography. (刺點畫廊; ☎852 2517 6238; www.blindspotgallery.com; 15th fl, Po Chai Industrial Bldg, 28 Wong Chuk Hang Rd, Aberdeen; ☉10am–6pm Tue-Sat, by appointment only Sun & Mon; ⊞70, 90, 590, 72, 42, 38)

Pok Fu Lam Village VILLAGE

7 ◉ Map p86, A1

Built on a sloping hillside, peaceful Pok Fu Lam Village looks like a shantytown compared to the high-density middle-class residences around it. Though no stunner, it's valued by historians not only for the famous fire dragon dance at the Mid-Autumn Festival, but equally for its ties to Hong Kong's dairy industry.

Other highlights include Bethanie and Li Ling Pagoda.As the sites are scattered, the best way to see them all is to join a walking tour. (薄扶林村; ☎852 6199 9473; www.pokfulamvillage.org; ⊞7, 40, 40M, 90B, 91)

Shek O Beach BEACH

8 ◉ Map p86, E3

Shek O beach has a large expanse of sand, shady trees to the rear, showers, changing facilities and lockers for rent. It's not quiet by any means, except on typhoon days, but the laid-back beach framed by rocky cliffs is quite pleasant. (石澳; ⊞9 from Shau Kei Wan MTR station, exit A3)

Eating

Aberdeen Fish Market Yee Hope Seafood Restaurant CANTONESE, SEAFOOD $$

9 ✗ Map p86, A2

Hidden in Hong Kong's only wholesale fish market, this understated eatery run by fishers is truly an in-the-know place for ultrafresh seafood. There's no menu, but tell them your budget and they'll source the best sea creatures available, including ones you don't normally see in restaurants, and apply their Midas touch to them. (香港仔魚市場二合海鮮餐廳; ☎852 5167 1819, 852 2177 7872; 102 Shek Pai Wan Rd, Aberdeen; meals from $350; ☉4am-4pm; ⊞107)

Ap Lei Chau Market Cooked Food Centre
SEAFOOD $

10 ✂ Map p86, A2

Above an indoor market, *dai pai dong* (food stall) operators cook up a storm in a sprawling hall littered with folding tables and plastic chairs. **Pak Kee** (栢記; ☎852 2555 2984; 1st fl, Ap Lei Chau Municipal Services Bldg,8 Hung Shing St, Ap Lei Chau; seafood dinner from HK$160; ⏱6pm-midnight; 🚐minibus 36X from Lee Garden Rd, Causeway Bay) and **Chu Kee** (珠記; ☎852 2555 2052; 1st fl, Ap Lei Chau Municipal Services Bldg, 8 Hung Shing St, Ap Lei Chau; seafood dinner from HK$160; ⏱6pm-midnight; 🚐minibus 36X from Lee Garden Rd, Causeway Bay) offer simple but tasty seafood dishes. You can also buy seafood from the wet market downstairs and pay them to cook it for you the way you want. It's packed

Local Life
Dairy Farm Tour

It was in Pok Fu Lam in 1886 that Dairy Farm (Map p86, A1) Hong Kong's first dairy was set up to provide the city with fresh milk. Offering employment to residents of Pok Fu Lam Village (p89), many of its physical structures, including dormitories and cowsheds, are still visible. Pok Fu Lam Village NGO runs tours of the area in Cantonese for HK$1500 per group, with an extra HK$300 for interpretation. See their Facebook page to book a month in advance.

and noisy on weekends. (鴨利洲市政大廈; 1st fl, Ap Lei Chau Municipal Services Bldg, 8 Hung Shing St, Ap Lei Chau; dishes HK$45-70; 🚐minibus 36X from Lee Garden Rd, Causeway Bay)

Hoi Kwong Seafood Restaurant
CANTONESE, SEAFOOD $

11 ✂ Map p86, B2

This hole-in-the-wall with sea life in tanks and styrofoam boxes at the entrance has a repertoire of a hundred-plus dishes, over half of which involve seafood. They keep prices down by not offering expensive and exotic varieties, but whatever they do have is always fresh and always local. Bookings essential. Be prepared to rub elbows with the next table. (海港食家; ☎852 2552 6463; 71 Ap Lei Chau Main St, Ap Lei Chau; mains HK$40-220; ⏱11.30am-2.30pm & 6-11.30pm)

Sei Yik
CANTONESE $

12 ✂ Map p86, D3

Weekenders flock to this small tin-roofed *dai pai dong* (food stall), right opposite the Stanley Municipal Building, for its fluffy Hong Kong–style French toast with *kaya* (coconut jam) spread. There's no English sign; look for the long queue of pilgrims and the piles of fruits that hide the entrance. (泗益; ☎852 2813 0507; 2 Stanley Market St, Stanley; meals from HK$30; ⏱6am-4pm Wed-Mon; 🚌6, 6A, 6X, 66)

Ap Lei Chau Market Cooked Food Centre

Drinking

Ben's Back Beach Bar BAR

13 Map p86, E3

Hidden on the quiet Shek O back beach, locals and expats munch burgers and sip cold brews beneath a rustic awning. A sea-facing shrine stands right next to this rugged ensemble. Enjoy reggae beats and the sound of the lapping waves while sipping beer. (石澳風帆會; ☎852 2809 2268; Shek O back beach, 273 Shek O Village; ⊙7pm-midnight Tue-Fri, 2pm-midnight Sat & Sun; ☒9 from Shau Kei Wan MTR station, exit A3)

Smugglers Inn PUB

14 Map p86, D3

When you're in an ever-renewing tourist hot spot like Stanley, it's nice to step into an institution like Smugglers Inn, where fads don't seem to have made an impact over the years. You can still have a Sex on the Beach next to its currency-plastered walls or outdoors on the waterfront, or play darts for free beers against fellow drinkers. There's even a jukebox. (☎852 2813 8852; Ground fl, 90A Stanley Main St, Stanley; ⊙10am-midnight Mon-Thu, to 1am Fri-Sun; ☒6, 6A, 6X or 260)

Understand

Fishing Culture in Aberdeen

Aberdeen Typhoon Shelter is where the sampans of the boat-dwelling fishermen used to moor. It was featured in many Hollywood films, including the second *Lara Croft: Tomb Raider* movie.

People of the Water

Most of the boat-dwellers belonged to the Tanka (蜑家人) ethnic group who arrived in Hong Kong from Southern China before the 10th century, and speak a dialect similar to Cantonese. Another group that lived here were the Hoklo (鶴佬) who originated in Fujian or Chiu Chow. The two groups did not always get along. The Tanka prefer to be called 'people of the water' (水上人) as 'Tanka' is a land-dwellers' term that they believe carries connotations of being uncivilised.

In 1961, the boat-dwelling population here stood at 28,000. Now only a few hundred remain. In *Tomb Raider: Cradle of Life*, families go about their idyllic lives in the harbour, but in reality, you'll see fishing junks next to luxury yachts, and speed-boats racing across the water.

Dragon Boat

There are fewer than 2000 fishing junks left in Aberdeen. Better-paying jobs on land have lured younger fishermen away from their traditional engagement. Despite this, the majority still see themselves as 'people of the water' and this identity is flaunted with fanfare at the dragon boat races held throughout the territory each year. On weekday evenings, teams practise in the typhoon shelter.

Hong Kong is the home of modern dragon boat racing. The city has the most teams (over 400) and the most races (over 20 a year) in the world per square metre. The most spectacular events during the racing season (March to October) are the fishermen's races which feature a combination of ritual and athleticism. The Dragon Boat Association (www.hkdba.com.hk) has listings.

LEUNGCHOPAN/SHUTTERSTOCK ©

Aberdeen Typhoon Shelter

Shopping

G.O.D.
CLOTHING, HOUSEWARES

15 🔒 Map p86, D3

One of the coolest born-in-Hong Kong shops around, G.O.D. does irreverent takes on classic Hong Kong iconography. Think cell phone covers printed with pictures of Hong Kong housing blocks, light fixtures resembling the ones in old-fashioned wet markets, and pillows covered in lucky koi print. There are a handful of G.O.D. shops in town, but this is one of the biggest. (Goods of Desire; 📞852 2673 0071; www.god.com.hk; Shop 105, Stanley Plaza, 22-23 Carmel Rd, Stanley; ⏰10.30am-8pm Mon-Fri, to 9pm Sat; 🚌6, 6A, 6X, 260)

Horizon Plaza
MALL

16 🔒 Map p86, A2

Tucked away on the southern coast of Ap Lei Chau, this enormous outlet housed in a converted factory building boasts more than 150 shops over 28 storeys. Most locals come here to buy furniture, but you'll also find Alexander McQueen on offer and Jimmy Choos at knock-down prices. Heaps of kiddies' stuff as well, from books and toys to clothing and furniture. (新海怡廣場; 2 Lee Wing St, Ap Lei Chau; ⏰10am-7pm; 🚌90 from Exchange Sq in Central)

Explore

Kowloon: Tsim Sha Tsui

Tsim Sha Tsui (TST), meaning 'sharp sandy point', is a vibrant district occupying the southern tip of the Kowloon Peninsula. Though best known for its shopping and dining, TST is also thick with museums and performance spaces. And with a population comprising Chinese, Indians, Filipinos, Nepalese, Africans and Europeans, it's Hong Kong's most cosmopolitan corner.

The Sights in a Day

Spend two hours at the **Museum of History** (p99), then stroll the scenic **Tsim Sha Tsui East Promenade** (p96) to the **Star Ferry Concourse**, stopping at the **Clock Tower** (p25) along the way. In between sights, indulge in Peking duck and unctuous Northern-style noodles at **Spring Deer** (p106).

Explore Tsim Sha Tsui's unique heritage at the **Former Marine Police Headquarters** (p99), **Fook Tak Ancient Temple** (p101), **Kowloon Mosque** (p102), **St Andrew's Anglican Church** (p101) and **Former Kowloon British School** (p101). End with afternoon tea at the **Peninsula** (p100) or samosas and lassi at **Chungking Mansions** across the road. Then head to **Harbour City** (p110) for retail therapy.

Wrap up your day with dinner at, Chicken HOF & Soju Korean (p105) followed by some of the town's best fruit cocktails at **Butler** (p108).

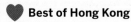

Top Sights

Tsim Sha Tsui
East Promenade (p96)

Best of Hong Kong

Eating
Woo Cow (p108)

Spring Deer (p106)

Ye Shanghai (p106)

Museums
Hong Kong
Museum of History (p99)

Hong Kong Museum of Art (p97)

June 4th Museum (p101)

Getting There

Ⓜ **Metro** Tsim Sha Tsui, exit E

Top Sights
Tsim Sha Tsui East Promenade

The resplendent views of Victoria Harbour make this walkway one of the best strolls in Hong Kong. Go during the day to take photos, visit the museums along the way and watch watercraft, lovers and tourists going about their business. After sundown, on your way to dinner or the Star Ferry, revisit the views, now magically transformed with skyscrapers decked out in neon robes.

尖沙嘴東部海濱花園

◉ Map p98 ,D4

Salisbury Rd, Tsim Sha Tsui

Ⓜ Tsim Sha Tsui, exit E

Avenue of the Stars

Clock Tower

A good place to begin your journey is at the Former Kowloon-Canton Railway (KCR) Clock Tower (p25) near the Star Ferry Concourse. The tower in red brick and granite, is a landmark of the age of steam. The clocks began ticking on 22 March 1921 and haven't stopped since, except during the Japanese occupation.

Museum of Art

This excellent **museum** (香港藝術館; ☎852 2721 0116; http://hk.art.museum; 10 Salisbury Rd, Tsim Sha Tsui; adult/concession HK$10/5, Wed free; ☉10am-6pm Mon-Fri, to 7pm Sat & Sun; ☺Star Ferry, Ⓜ East Tsim Sha Tsui, exit J) is currently closed as it undergoes a multimillion-dollar renovation. When open, it has seven galleries spread over six floors exhibiting contemporary Hong Kong art, Chinese antiquities, and historical pictures.

Avenue of the Stars

Passing the Cultural Centre and the Museum of Art, you'll arrive at the Avenue of Stars, Hong Kong's lacklustre tribute to its once-brilliant film industry. The highlight here is a 2.5m tall bronze statue of kung fu icon Bruce Lee. Most of this area is closed for renovation until late 2018. Stairs and a lift, just past the Avenue of the Stars, lead to the handsome Tsim Sha Tsui East Podium Garden and Middle Road Children's Playground (p102).

Symphony of Lights

Every single evening from the promenade you can watch the Symphony of Lights (Kowloon waterfront; ☉8-8.20pm)**,** a kitschy but classic light and music show that takes place at 8pm, with classical Chinese songs playing in time to the sight of the Hong Kong Island skyscrapers flashing their lights across the harbour.

☑ Top Tips

▶ There's not much to eat on the waterfront itself, so fortify yourself beforehand.

▶ The Avenue of Stars section of the Tsim Sha Tsui East Promenade – roughly from just outside the Space Museum at 10 Salisbury Rd for 400m northeast along the coast – is closed for a makeover until 2018.

▶ Beware of con artists in monk outfits – real monks never solicit money. Some try to sell Buddhist amulets, or force 'blessings' on you then pester you for a donation. When accosted, just say 'no' firmly and ignore them.

✗ Take a Break

▶ Stop for a cocktail with million-dollar views at the InterContinental Lobby Lounge (p109).

▶ Finish your walk with a hearty south Indian meal at Woodlands (p108), in East Tsim Sha Tsui.

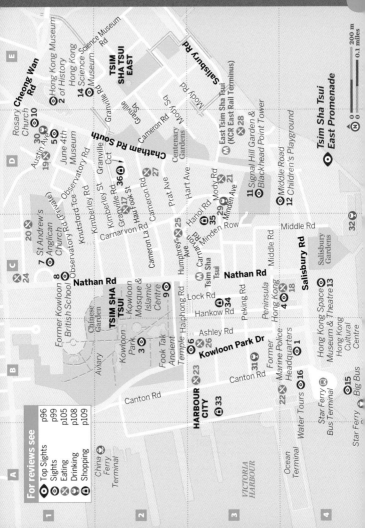

For reviews see

◉	Top Sights	p96
◉	Sights	p99
⊗	Eating	p105
◐	Drinking	p108
◐	Shopping	p109

Junks (traditional Chinese sailing ships) at Hong Kong Museum of History

Sights

Former Marine Police
Headquarters   HISTORIC BUILDING

1 ⊙ Map p98, B4

Built in 1884, this gorgeous Victorian complex is one of Hong Kong's four oldest government buildings. It was used continuously by the Hong Kong Marine Police, except during WWII when the Japanese navy took over. The complex is now a nakedly commercial property called 'Heritage 1881'. Some of the old structures are still here, including stables, pigeon houses and bomb shelter. Why 1881? Because '4' has a similar pronunciation to 'death' in Chinese, and the developer was superstitious. (前水警總部; ☑852 2926 8000, tour reservation 852 2926 1881; www.1881heritage.com; 2A Canton Rd, Tsim Sha Tsui; admission free; ⊘10am-10pm; ⚓Star Ferry, ⓂEast Tsim Sha Tsui, exit L6)

Hong Kong
Museum of History   MUSEUM

2 ⊙ Map p98, E1

For a whistle-stop overview of the territory's archaeology, ethnography, and natural and local history, this museum is well worth a visit, not just to learn more about the subject but also to understand how Hong Kong presents its stories to the world. 'The Hong Kong Story' takes visitors through the territory's past via eight

EWILDING/SHUTTERSTOCK ©

Bamboo arch at Kowloon Park

galleries, starting with the natural environment and prehistoric Hong Kong – about 6000 years ago, give or take a lunar year – and ending with the territory's return to China in 1997. (香港歷史博物館; ☏852 2724 9042; http://hk.history.museum; 100 Chatham Rd South, Tsim Sha Tsui; adult/concession HK$10/5, Wed free; ◷10am-6pm Mon & Wed-Sat, to 7pm Sun; ♿; Ⓜ Tsim Sha Tsui, exit B2)

Kowloon Park
PARK

3 ◎ Map p98, B2

Built on the site of a barracks for Indian soldiers in the colonial army, Kowloon Park is an oasis of greenery and a refreshing escape from the hustle and bustle of Tsim Sha Tsui. Pathways

and walls criss-cross the grass, birds hop around in cages, and ancient banyan trees dot the landscape. In the morning the older set practise taichi amid the serene surrounds, and on Sunday afternoon Kung Fu Corner stages martial-arts displays. (九龍公園; www.lcsd.gov.hk; Nathan & Austin Rds, Tsim Sha Tsui; ◷6am-midnight; ♿; Ⓜ Tsim Sha Tsui, exit C2)

Peninsula Hong Kong
HISTORIC BUILDING

4 ◎ Map p98, C4

The Peninsula (c 1928), housed in a throne-like building, is one of the world's great hotels. Once called 'the finest hotel east of Suez', the Pen was one of several prestigious hotels across Asia, lining up with (but not behind) the likes of the Raffles in Singapore and the Cathay (now the Peace) in Shànghǎi. Taking afternoon tea here is a wonderful experience – dress neatly and be prepared to queue for a table. (香港半島酒店; www.peninsula.com; cnr Salisbury & Nathan Rds, Tsim Sha Tsui; Ⓜ East Tsim Sha Tsui, exit L3)

June 4th Museum
MUSEUM

5 Map p98, D1

The world's first permanent museum dedicated to the 1989 pro-democracy protests in Běijīng's Tiān'ānmén Square. The 800-sq-ft space has artefacts, photographs, books and microfilm related to the incident including casings of bullets supposedly fired by the People's Liberation Army and T-shirts signed by the Běijīng student leaders, including Wang Dan. A copy of the *Goddess of Democracy* statue built by the students stands at the heart of the museum. (六四紀念館; ☎852 2782 6111; http://64museum.blogspot.hk; 5th fl, Foo Hoo Centre, 3 Austin Ave, Tsim Sha Tsui; adult/concession HK$20/10; ◷10am-6pm Mon & Wed-Fri, to 7pm Sat & Sun; Ⓜ Jordan, exit D)

Fook Tak Ancient Temple
BUDDHIST TEMPLE

6 Map p98, B3

Tsim Sha Tsui's only temple is a smoke-filled hole in the wall with a hot tin roof. Little is known about its ancestry except that it was built

as a shrine in the Qing dynasty and renovated in 1900. Before WWII, worshippers of its Earth God were the unskilled labourers from Kowloon Wharf nearby, where the Ocean Terminal now stands. Today most incense offerers are octogenarians – the temple specialises in longevity. (福德古廟; 30 Haiphong Rd, Tsim Sha Tsui; ◷6am-8pm; Ⓜ Tsim Sha Tsui, exit C2)

St Andrew's Anglican Church
CHURCH

7 Map p98, C1

Sitting atop a knoll, next to the Former Kowloon British School, is this charming building in English Gothic style that houses Kowloon's oldest Protestant church. St Andrew's was built in 1905 in granite and red brick to serve Kowloon's Protestant population; it was turned into a Shinto shrine during the Japanese Occupation. Nearby you'll see the handsome former vicarage with columned balconies (c 1909). Enter from the eastern side of Nathan Rd via steps or a slope. (聖安德烈堂; ☎852 2367 1478; www.standrews.org.hk; 138 Nathan Rd, Tsim Sha Tsui; ◷7.30am-10.30pm, church 8.30am-5.30pm; Ⓜ Tsim Sha Tsui, exit B1)

Former Kowloon British School
HISTORIC BUILDING

8 Map p98, C1

The oldest surviving school building for expat children is a listed Victorian-style structure that now houses the Antiquities and Monuments Office

(古物古蹟辦事處). Established in 1902, it was subsequently modified to incorporate breezy verandahs and high ceilings, prompted possibly by the fainting spells suffered by its young occupants. (前九龍英童學校; www.amo.gov.hk; 136 Nathan Rd, Tsim Sha Tsui; Ⓜ Tsim Sha Tsui, exit B1)

Kowloon Mosque & Islamic Centre

MOSQUE

9 ◉ Map p98, C2

This structure, with its dome and carved marble, is Hong Kong's largest mosque. It serves the territory's 70,000-odd Muslims, more than half of whom are Chinese, and accommodates up to 3000 worshippers. The mosque was originally established to serve the Indian Muslim troops of the British army who were stationed at what is now Kowloon Park. Muslims are welcome to attend services, but non-Muslims should ask permission to enter. Remember to remove your footwear. (九龍清真寺; ☎ 852 2724 0095; 105 Nathan Rd, Tsim Sha Tsui; ⊙ 5am-10pm; Ⓜ Tsim Sha Tsui, exit C2)

Rosary Church

CHURCH

10 ◉ Map p98, D1

Kowloon's oldest Catholic church was built in 1905 with money donated by a Portuguese doctor in Hong Kong, initially for the benefit of the Catholics in an Indian battalion stationed in Kowloon, and later for the burgeoning local Catholic community. Rosary Church features a classic Gothic style

with a yellowish facade reminiscent of churches in Macau. (玫瑰堂; ☎ 852 2368 0980; http://rosarychurch.catholic. org.hk; 125 Chatham Rd S, Tsim Sha Tsui; ⊙ 7.30am-7.30pm; Ⓜ Jordan, exit D)

Signal Hill Garden & Blackhead Point Tower

PARK

11 ◉ Map p98, D3

The views from the top of this knoll are quite spectacular, and if it were the 1900s the ships in the harbour might be returning your gaze – a copper ball in the handsome Edwardian-style tower was dropped at 1pm daily so seafarers could adjust their chronometers. The garden is perched above the Middle Road Children's Playground (p102). Enter from Minden Row (Mody Rd). (訊號山公園和訊號塔; Minden Row, Tsim Sha Tsui; ⊙ tower 9-11am & 4-6pm; Ⓜ East Tsim Sha Tsui, exit K)

Middle Road Children's Playground

PARK

12 ◉ Map p98, D4

Accessible via a sweep of stairs from Chatham Rd South, this hidden gem atop the East Tsim Sha Tsui MTR station has play facilities, shaded seating and views of the waterfront. On weekdays it's the quiet backyard playground of the residents nearby, but on weekends it's filled with children and picnickers of as many ethnicities as there are ways to go down a slide (if you're eight). (中間道兒童遊樂場; Middle Rd, Tsim Sha Tsui; ⊙ 7am-11pm; 🚻; Ⓜ East Tsim Sha Tsui, exit K)

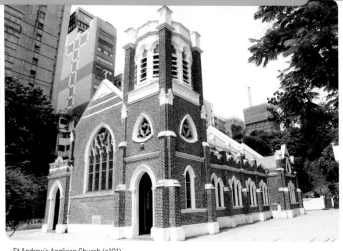

St Andrew's Anglican Church (p101)

Hong Kong Space Museum & Theatre
MUSEUM

13 Map p98, C4

This golf-ball–shaped building on the waterfront houses two exhibition halls and a planetarium with a large screen on the ceiling. The museum has a dated feel, but the Omnimax films, the virtual paraglider and the 'moon-walking' simulator hold a timeless fascination for kidults. The museum shop also sells dehydrated 'astronaut' ice cream in three flavours. (香港太空館; ☎852 2721 0226; www.lcsd.gov.hk; 10 Salisbury Rd, Tsim Sha Tsui; adult/concession HK$10/5, shows HK$24/12, Wed free; ⏰1-9pm Mon & Wed-Fri, 10am-9pm Sat & Sun; 👶; Ⓜ East Tsim Sha Tsui, exit J)

Hong Kong Science Museum
MUSEUM

14 Map p98, E1

Illustrating the fundamental workings of technology, with practical demonstrations of the laws of energy, physics and chemistry, the Hong Kong Science Museum is a great hands-on experience capable of entertaining adults as well as children from toddlers to teens. (香港科學館; ☎852 2732 3232; http://hk.science.museum; 2 Science Museum Rd, Tsim Sha Tsui; adult/concession HK$25/12.50, Wed free; ⏰10am-7pm Mon-Wed & Fri, to 9pm Sat & Sun; 👶; Ⓜ Tsim Sha Tsui, exit B2)

SAIKO3P/SHUTTERSTOCK ©

Traditional junk boat harbour tour

Big Bus Company
BUS

15 ◉ Map p98, B4

A good way to get your bearings in the city is on the hop-on, hop-off, open-topped double-deckers. Three tours are available: the Kowloon Route takes in much of the Tsim Sha Tsui and Hung Hom waterfront; the Hong Kong Island Route explores Central, Admiralty, Wan Chai and Causeway Bay; and the Green Tour goes to Stanley Market and Aberdeen. (☏852 3102 9021; www.bigbustours.com; Unit KP-38, 1st fl, Star Ferry Pier, Tsim Sha Tsui; adult/child from HK$450/400; ☺9am-6pm)

Water Tours
BOATING

16 ◉ Map p98, B4

Offers six different tours of the harbour on junk-style boats, as well as dinner and cocktail cruises. Prices range from HK$260 (HK$170 for children aged two to 12 years) for the Morning Harbour Cruise, to HK$350 (HK$260 for children) for the Symphony of Lights Cruise and HK$900 (HK$700 for children) for the Aberdeen Dinner Cruise. (☏852 2926 3868; www.watertours.com.hk; 6th fl Carnarvon Plaza, 20 Carnarvon Rd, Tsim Sha Tsui)

Eating

Yum Cha

DIM SUM $

17 Map p98, D2

Adorable, animal-shaped dumplings and buns are just begging to be Instagrammed at Yum Cha, one of the newer players on Hong Kong's dim-sum scene. Barbecue pork buns are adorned with tiny piggy faces, custard buns are anthropomorphic eggs, and bird-shaped pineapple puffs are served in ornate cages. There's also a full menu of Cantonese fare, rendered with a modern twist. (飲茶; ☎852 2751 1666; http://yumchahk.com; 3/F 20-22 Granville Rd, Tsim Sha Tsui; meals HK$100-250; ⏱11.30am-3pm & 6-11pm; Ⓜ Tsim Sha Tsui, exit B2)

Gaddi's

FRENCH $$$

18 Map p98, C4

Gaddi's, which opened just after WWII, was the kind of place where wealthy families went to celebrate special occasions. Today the classical decor may be a tad stuffy and the live Filipino band gratuitous, but the food – traditional French with contemporary touches – is without a doubt still some of the best in town. (☎852 2696 6763; www.peninsula.com; 1st fl, The Peninsula, 19-21 Salisbury Rd, Tsim Sha Tsui; set lunch/dinner HK$500/2000; ⏱noon-2.30pm & 7-10.30pm; Ⓜ Tsim Sha Tsui, exit E)

Chicken HOF & Soju Korean

KOREAN $

19 Map p98, D1

This place with darkened windows may look dodgy from the outside, but in fact it's a Korean gastropub with a friendly owner who'll holler a greeting when customers enter. The excellent fried chicken, made with a light and crispy batter, comes in five versions. Traditional fare such as Korean barbecue is also available. If you need to ask directions, locals often refer to this place as 'Lee Family Chicken'. A long queue is the norm. (李家; Chicken; ☎852 2375 8080; Ground fl, 84 Kam Kok Mansion, Kimberley Rd, Tsim Sha Tsui; meals from HK$150; ⏱5pm-4am; Ⓜ Jordan, exit D)

Local Life
Multicultural Kowloon

Ethnic pockets abound in Kowloon, especially in Tsim Sha Tsui, which means food options are diverse and often excitingly so. Head to the streets around Chungking Mansions (p110) to find the best Indian grocery stores; Kimberley St and Austin Ave for Korean restaurants and minimarts; the streets around Temple Street Night Market (p114) in Yau Ma Tei for Nepalese curries; and Kowloon City for authentic Thai eateries and grocery stores.

Yoga Interactive Vegetarian
VEGETARIAN, ASIAN $

20 🍴 Map p98, C1

The Asian vegetarian meals here, cooked by a yoga teacher, are among the best in town. But you'll need to book at least a week in advance. That said, if there's only one or two of you, they might be able to fit you in sooner. This homey place is one flight of stairs above the 14th floor. (互動瑜伽素食; ☎852 3422 1195, 852 9327 7275; www.yogafitnesshk.com; 30 Hillwood Rd, 15B Changlin Ct, Tsim Sha Tsui; meals HK$200; ⊙noon-3pm & 7-10pm; 🍴; Ⓜ Jordan, exit D)

Spring Deer
PEKING DUCK $$

21 🍴 Map p98, D3

Hong Kong's most authentic northern-style roasted lamb is served here. Better known is the Peking duck, which is very good. That said, the service can be about as welcoming as a Běijīng winter, c 1967. Booking is essential. (鹿鳴春飯店; ☎852 2366 4012; 1st fl, 42 Mody Rd, Tsim Sha Tsui; meals HK$80-500; ⊙noon-3pm & 6-11pm; Ⓜ East Tsim Sha Tsui, exit N2)

Yè Shanghai
DIM SUM $$

22 🍴 Map p98, B4

The name means 'Shànghǎi Nights'. Dark woods and subtle lighting inspired by 1920s Shànghǎi fill the air with romance. The modern Shanghainese dishes are also exquisite. The only exception to this Jiāngnán harmony is the Cantonese dim sum being served at lunch, though that too is wonderful. Sophisticated Yè Shanghai has one Michelin star. (夜上海; ☎852 2376 3322; www.elite-concepts.com; 6th fl, Marco Polo Hotel, Harbour City, Canton Rd, Tsim Sha Tsui; meals HK$400-800; ⊙11.30am-2.30pm & 6-10.30pm; 🍴; Ⓜ Tsim Sha Tsui, exit C2)

Din Tai Fung
TAIWANESE, NOODLES $$

23 🍴 Map p98, B3

Whether it's comfort food or a carb fix you're craving, the juicy Shanghai dumplings and hearty northern-style noodles at this beloved Taiwanese chain will do the trick. Queues are the norm and there are no reservations, but service is excellent. Must-eats include the famous *xiao long bao* (soup dumplings), fluffy steamed pork buns and the greasy-but-oh-so-good fried pork chop. (鼎泰豐; ☎852 2730 6928; www.dintaifung.com.hk; Shop 130, 3rd fl, Silvercord, 30 Canton Rd, Tsim Sha Tsui; meals HK$120-300; ⊙11.30am-10.30pm; 🍴; Ⓜ Tsim Sha Tsui, exit C1)

Hing Kee Restaurant
CANTONESE $$

24 🍴 Map p98, C1

This celebrity haunt is run by a feisty fisherman's daughter who's known for her brilliant dishes prepared the way they were on sampans. The signature crabs smothered in a mountain of fried garlic are a wonder to taste and behold. The service can be a little edgy. Be sure you know the price of every dish before you order. (避風塘興記; ☎852 2722 0022; 1st fl, Bowa House, 180 Nathan Rd, Tsim Sha Tsui; meals HK$380-1200; ⊙6pm-5am; Ⓜ Jordan, exit D)

BUSHTON3/GETTY IMAGES ©

Classic Hong Kong fare of Cha siu bao

Mammy Pancake DESSERTS $

25 Map p98, C2

This takeaway counter serves up some of Hong Kong's best eggettes, the egg-shaped waffles beloved by local children and adults alike. Get them in classic plain, or in inventive flavours such as green tea, chestnut, sweet potato or pork floss. Or pig out with a waffle sandwich oozing with peanut butter and condensed milk. Expect a 15-minute wait for your treat. (媽咪雞蛋仔; 8-12 Carnarvon Rd, Tsim Sha Tsui; egg waffles HK$16-28; ⏰11.30am-9pm Sun-Thu, to 10.30pm Fri & Sat; Ⓜ Tsim Sha Tsui, exit D2)

Tak Fat Beef Balls NOODLES $

26 Map p98, B3

This famous *dai pai dong* (food stall) is one of a handful operating in the Haiphong Rd Temporary Market. Pick a seat in the cacophonous sprawl and order the beef ball noodles, famed for their bounce and hint of dried mandarin peel. The market is next door to Fook Tak Ancient Temple. Venture past the florists and halal meat stalls to reach the *dai pai dong*. (德發牛肉丸; Haiphong Rd, Tsim Sha Tsui; beef ball noodles HK$28; ⏰9am-8pm; Ⓜ Tsim Sha Tsui, exit A1)

Woo Cow

HOTPOT $$

27 Map p98, D2

Indecisive gluttons will scream at the mind-blowing hotpot choices here – 200 ingredients (the majority fresh or homemade), 20 kinds of broth (from clam soup to fancy herbal concoctions) and an embarrassment of condiments (all-you-can-dip)! There's no escaping the menu either – the lights are too bright! Now onto the sashimi options... Booking essential. (禾牛薈火焗館; Great Beef Hot Pot; ☑852 3997 3369; 1st & 2nd fl, China Insurance Bldg, 48 Cameron Rd, Tsim Sha Tsui; meals HK$350-600; ⏱5.30pm-2am; Ⓜ Tsim Sha Tsui, exit B3)

Woodlands

INDIAN $

28 Map p98, D3

Located above a department store, good old Woodlands offers excellent-value Indian vegetarian food to compatriots and the odd local. Dithering gluttons should order the *thali* meal, which is served on a round metal plate with 10 tiny dishes, a dessert and bread. Dosai are excellent. (活蘭印度素食; ☑852 2369 3718; Upper ground fl, 16 & 17 Wing On Plaza, 62 Mody Rd, Tsim Sha Tsui; meals HK$70-180; ⏱noon-3.30pm & 6.30-10.30pm; 🖉🛗; Ⓜ East Tsim Sha Tsui, exit P1)

Drinking

Butler

COCKTAIL BAR

29 Map p98, D3

A cocktail and whisky heaven hidden in the residential part of Tsim Sha Tsui. You can flip through its whisky magazines as you watch the experienced bartenders create magical concoctions with the flair and precision of a master mixologist in Ginza. We loved the cocktails made from fresh citruses. A discreet and welcome addition to the Tsim Sha Tsui drinking scene. (☑852 2724 3828; 5th fl, Mody House, 30 Mody Rd, Tsim Sha Tsui; drinks around HK$200; ⏱6.30pm-3am Mon-Fri, to 2am Sat & Sun; Ⓜ East Tsim Sha Tsui, exit N2)

Amuse

BAR

30 Map p98, D1

An airy bistro-like bar frequented by white-collar locals and university students who come for their draught beers, decent wines and funky cocktails. The best seats are the leather couches next to a row of large windows; the communal table is great if you want to meet people, and the banquettes make for intimate tête-à-têtes. (☑852 2317 1988; 4 Austin Ave, Tsim Sha Tsui; ⏱5pm-4am Mon-Fri, 6pm-4am Sat, 6pm-3am Sun; 🛜; Ⓜ Jordan, exit D)

Aqua

BAR

31 Map p98, B3

When night falls, you'll know why this uberfashionable bar has dim illumination and black furniture – the two-storey, floor-to-ceiling windows command sweeping views of the Hong Kong Island skyline that come to life after sundown. The tables by the windows are awesome for bringing a date. On the weekends, a DJ spins hip hop

Chungking Mansions (p110)

and lounge jazz. (☎ 852 3427 2288; www. aqua.com.hk; 29 & 30th fl, 1 Peking Rd, Tsim Sha Tsui; ⏲ 4pm-2am, happy hour 4-6pm; 🛜; Ⓜ Tsim Sha Tsui, exit L5)

InterContinental Lobby Lounge
BAR

32 Map p98, C4

Soaring plate glass and an unbeatable waterfront location make this one of the best spots to soak up the Hong Kong Island skyline and take in the busy harbour, although you pay for the privilege. It's also an ideal venue from which to watch the evening light show at 8pm. (☎ 852 2721 1211; www.hongkong-ic.intercontinental.com; Hotel InterContinental Hong Kong, 18 Salisbury Rd, Tsim Sha Tsui; ⏲ 7am-12.30am; 🛜; Ⓜ East Tsim Sha Tsui, exit J)

Shopping

Initial
CLOTHING

This attractive shop and cafe (see 27 ❌ Map p98, D2) carries stylish, multifunctional urbanwear with European and Japanese influences. The clothes created by local designers are complemented by imported shoes, bags and costume jewellery. (www. initialfashion.com; Shop 2, 48 Cameron Rd, Tsim Sha Tsui; ⏲ 11.30am-11.30pm; Ⓜ Tsim Sha Tsui, exit B2)

Harbour City
MALL

33 🔒 Map p98, B3

This is an enormous place, with 700 shops, 50 food and beverage outlets and five cinemas. Outlets are arrayed in four separate zones: for kids, sport, fashion, and cosmetics and beauty. Almost every major brand is represented. Massively crowded on weekends. (www.harbourcity.com.hk; 3-9 Canton Rd, Tsim Sha Tsui; ⏱10am-10pm; MTsim Sha Tsui, exit C1)

Swindon Books
BOOKS

34 🔒 Map p98, C3

This is one of the best locally run bookshops in the city, with an excellent range and knowledgeable staff. Strong on local books and history in particular. (☑852 2366 8001; www.swindonbooks.com/; 13-15 Lock Rd, Tsim Sha Tsui; ⏱9am-6pm Mon-Fri, to 1pm Sat; MTsim Sha Tsui, exit A1)

K11 Select
ACCESSORIES, CLOTHING

35 🔒 Map p98, C3

In the **K11** (18 Hanoi Rd, Tsim Sha Tsui; MEast Tsim Sha Tsui, exit D2) mall, this shop gathers the best of Hong Kong designers in one spot. Look for theatrical clothing from Daydream Nation, founded by a pair of Hong Kong siblings, and unisex accessories from Kapok. (Shop 101, K11 Mall, 18 Hanoi Rd, Tsim Sha Tsui; ⏱10am-10pm)

Rise Shopping Arcade
CLOTHING

36 🔒 Map p98, D2

Bursting the seams of this minimall is cheap streetwear from Hong Kong, Korea and Japan, with a few knock-offs chucked in for good measure. Patience and a good eye could land you purchases fit for a Vogue photo shoot. It's best visited between 4pm and 8.30pm when most of the shops are open. (利時商場; 5-11 Granville Circuit, Tsim Sha Tsui; ⏱3-9pm; MTsim Sha Tsui, exit B2)

Ⓠ Local Life
Poor Man's Peninsula

Say 'budget accommodation' and 'Hong Kong' in one breath and everyone thinks of Chungking Mansions (CKM). Built in 1961 just across Nathan Rd from the Peninsula (Map p98, C3), CKM is a labyrinth of homes, guesthouses, Indian restaurants, souvenir stalls and foreign-exchange shops spread over five 17-storey blocks. According to anthropologist Gordon Mathews, it has a resident population of about 4000 and an estimated 10,000 daily visitors. More than 120 different nationalities pass through its doors in a single year.

It's fun to visit CKM just to feel the vibe and shop – the South Asian grocery stores, Indian boutiques selling pretty costume jewellery, and Indian restaurants are recommended. Touts will try to sell you everything from 'copy watch' to mystery herbs. It's best to ignore them, though some may just be trying to bring you to their restaurant.

Movie buffs note: it was at nearby Mirador Mansion – not Chungking Mansions – that Wong Kar-wai filmed most of *Chungking Express* (1994).

Understand

The ABCs of Tao

If you see temples guarded by fierce-looking gods, they are likely to be Taoist temples. Taoism is an indigenous religion that originated in the shamanistic roots of Chinese civilisation. Though never declared a national religion, its influence has been ubiquitous in Chinese life from the Tang to Ming dynasties. Unlike evangelical religions stressing crusading and conversion, Taoism addresses practical needs such as cures for illnesses, protection from evil spirits and funerary requirements.

Tao for the Road

Construction projects are always preceded by a ritual to appease nature deities such as the Earth God. Offerings of fruit are piled on a makeshift shrine and incense sticks are lit. Similar rituals take place before the shooting of a film or the opening of a shop. Keeping the deities happy is important for health, safety and feng shui, the last a belief influenced by Taoism.

Tao for the Dead

The majority of funeral rites in Hong Kong are presided over by Taoist 'ritual specialists'. More colourful than Buddhist ceremonies, Taoist rites feature the chanting of scriptures to the striking of a wooden hand-held slit drum called *muyu*, and fanciful procedures that may include the sprinkling of flowers to relieve bitterness.

Taoist Temples

In the first two weeks of the Lunar New Year, millions in Hong Kong pay their respects at Taoist temples. These tend to be more decorative than Buddhist places of worship, and there are no nuns or monks, only ritual specialists, who can marry and have children.

Explore

Kowloon: Yau Ma Tei & Mong Kok

Yau Ma Tei – meaning the place (*tei*) where fishermen waterproofed boats with oil (*yau*) and repaired hemp ropes (*ma*) – rewards the explorer with a close look at a more traditional Hong Kong. Congested Mong Kok (Prosperous Point) teems with shops selling electronics, clothes, jewellery and kitchen supplies, but a few cultural oases have also emerged in the area.

The Sights in a Day

 Have breakfast at **Mido Café** (p120) in Yau Ma Tei. Replenished, explore **Tin Hau Temple** (p118), the **Jade Market** (p122), and then stroll down **Shanghai Street** (p118), poking your head into the traditional shops. All this should take around two hours.

 Have a light and tasty lunch at **Nathan Congee and Noodle** (p120). Head north towards Mong Kok to visit the beautiful and historic **Lui Seng Chun** (p117) building and art gallery, **C&G Artpartment** (p117). If there's time, rummage for quirky gifts and souvenirs at Mong Kok's mini-malls, such as **Yue Hwa Chinese Emporium** (p123).

🌙 Dine under the stars at **Temple Street Night Market** (p114). Then it's on to **Canton Singing House** (p122) for some old-fashioned Hong Kong-style revelry.

 Top Sights

Temple Street
Night Market (p114)

 Best of Hong Kong

Shopping

Yue Hwa Chinese
Products Emporium (p123)

Chan Wah Kee Cutlery (p122)

Markets

Temple Street
Night Market (p114)

Wholesale Fruit Market (p118)

Ladies' Market (p122)

Getting There

Ⓜ **Metro** Jordan, Yau Ma Tei and Mong Kok stations (Tsuen Wanline).

🚌 **Bus** Buses 2, 6, 6A and 9.

Top Sights
Temple Street Night Market

The liveliest night market in Hong Kong, Temple St extends from Man Ming Lane to Nanking Stand and is cut in two by Tin Hau Temple. It's a great place to go for the bustling atmosphere, the smells and tastes from the food stalls, the occasional Cantonese opera performance, and some shopping and fortune telling.

廟街夜市

◉ Map p116, B4

Temple St, Yau Ma Tei

🕘 6-11pm

Ⓜ Yau Ma Tei, exit C

Shopping

While you may find better bargains further north in Kowloon, it's fun to shop here. The stalls are crammed with cheap clothes, watches, footwear, cookware and everyday items. Any marked prices should be considered suggestions – this is definitely a place to bargain.

Street Food

For al fresco dining head to Woo Sung St, which runs parallel to the east, or to the section of Temple St north of the temple. You can get anything from a bowl of noodles to Chiu Chow–style oyster omelette, costing anywhere from HK$30 to HK$300. There are also quite a few seafood and hotpot restaurants in the area.

Fortune Telling

Every evening a gaggle of fortune tellers sets up tents in the middle of the market where they make predictions about your life (for HK$100 up) by reading your face, palm or based on your date of birth. Some keep birds that have been trained to pick out 'fortune' cards. Most operators speak some English.

Temple Street's Singalong Parlours

A highlight of Yau Ma Tei is its old-fashioned singalong parlours (歌廳). These originated 20 years ago to offer shelter to street singers on rainy days.

Most parlours have basic set-ups – tables, a stage and Christmas lights for an upbeat atmosphere. All have their own organist and a troupe of freelance singers – women who'll keep you company and persuade you to make a dedication or sing along with them for a fee. Their repertoire ranges from Chinese operatic extracts to English oldies. You'll see many regulars at these places – kooky types from the neighbourhood; older men who drink from whisky flasks and know all the dames...

☑ Top Tips

▶ While the majority of sellers have no price tags on their goods, some do. Use those to gain an idea of what a semi-reasonable price might be before bargaining at tag-less stalls.

▶ Touts will try to hustle you to their seafood stalls – no need to resist, as they're pretty much all the same.

▶ The market is at its best from 7pm to 10pm, when it's clogged with stalls and people.

✗ Take a Break

▶ If you're not going to eat at one of the market's *dai pai dongs* (food stalls), stop in at **Osama Tony** (☏ 852 2755 5090; 122 Woo Sung St, Jordan; meals HK$40-80; ⏱ noon-11pm; Ⓜ Jordan, exit A) for cheap *xiao long bao* (soup dumplings) and crispy radish cakes.

▶ Snag a pre-bedtime snack of milk tea and egg toast at Australia Dairy Company (p119).

Larch St
Fuk Tsum St
Ivy St

Tong Mi Rd

Anchor St
Park

OLYMPIC CITY

West Kowloon Corridor West

HOI FU COURT

Lai Cheung Rd

Lin Cheung Rd

Hoi Wang Rd

Man Cheong St
Man Wai St
Man Ying St
Man Wui St
Wai Ching St
Ferry St

Jordan Rd

Austin

Canton Rd

Bute St
MONG KOK
Canton Rd
Mong Kok Rd
Fife St

Nathan Rd
Sai Yeung Choi St South

2

C&G Artpartment 1

Mong Kok

Argyle St

Nelson St
Shantung St
Soy St
Shanghai St
Portland St
Nathan Rd
Tung On St
Pitt St
Hamilton St
Tung Fong St

18

Dundas St

9

7 Yau Ma Tei

Wholesale Fruit Market 5
Shek Lung St
Man Ming La

YAU MA TEI

Shanghai Street 3
13
14
10
16
Kansu St
Canton Rd
Battery St
Reclamation St
Pak Hoi St
Shanghai St
Saigon St
Temple St
Ning Po St
Woo Sung St
Nanking St

Temple Street Night Market
Temple St

Tin Hau Temple
4

19

11

15 6
Bowring St
12 Jordan

Jordan Rd
Chi Wo St

Mong Kok East

Kadoorie Av

Argyle St

Sai Yee St
Yim Po Fong St
Peace Ave
Soares Ave
Victory Ave

Man Fuk Rd

17
Macpherson Playground

Kwong Wa St

Waterloo Rd

Wylie Rd

Princess Margaret Rd
Chung Hau St

King's Park

KING'S PARK

King's Par Sports Ground

Gascoigne Rd

0   400 m
0   0.25 miles

N

For reviews see	
⊙ Top Sights	p114
⊙ Sights	p117
⊗ Eating	p119
⊖ Drinking	p121
⊕ Entertainment	p122
⊡ Shopping	p122

STEVECIMAGES/GETTY IMAGES ©

Lui Seng Chun

Sights

C&G Artpartment GALLERY

1 ⊙ Map p116, B1

Clara and Gum, the founders of this edgy art space behind the Pioneer Centre (始創中心), are passionate about nurturing the local art scene and representing socially minded artists. They close late when there are events. See website for the latest. (☎852 2390 9332; www.candg-artpartment. com; 3rd fl, 222 Sai Yeung Choi St S, Mong Kok; ⊙2-7.30pm Thu, Fri, Sun & Mon, from 11am Sat; Ⓜ Prince Edward, exit B2)

Lui Seng Chun HISTORIC BUILDING

2 ⊙ Map p116, B1

Hugging a street corner is this beautiful four-storey Chinese 'shophouse' belonging to a school of Chinese medicine. Constructed circa 1931, it features a mix of Chinese and European architectural styles – deep verandahs, urn-shaped balustrades and other fanciful takes on a neoclassical Italian villa. The ground floor, which has a herbal tea shop, is open to the public. Free guided tours to the upper-floor clinics is available by registration. They're in Cantonese, but exhibits have bilingual labels. (雷春生堂; ☎852 3411 0628; http://scm.hkbu.edu.hk/lsctour; 119 Lai Chi Kok Rd, cnr Tong Mi Rd, Mong

Kok; admission free; ⊙ guided tour 2.30pm & 4pm Mon-Fri, 9.30am & 11am Sat, consultation 9am-1pm & 2-8pm Mon-Sat, 9am-1pm Sun; Ⓜ Prince Edward, exit C2)

Shanghai Street   STREET

3 ⊙ Map p116, B4

Strolling down Shanghai St will take you back to a time long past. Once Kowloon's main drag, it's flanked by stores selling Chinese wedding gowns, sandalwood incense and Buddha statues, as well as mah-jong parlours and an old pawn shop (at the junction with Saigon St). This is a terrific place for souvenirs – fun picks include wooden mooncake moulds stamped with images of fish or pigs or lucky sayings, bamboo

Local Life
Getting Inked in Hong Kong

Tattoo artist **Nic Tse** (美華刺青; ☑ 852 2757 0027, 852 6333 5352; kowloonink@gmail.com; 4th fl, 703 Shanghai St, Mong Kok; per hr HK$1000; Ⓜ Prince Edward, exit C1) has a repertoire that includes abstract contemporary designs, lines of poetry and minimalist armscapes. Interested parties should email him as early as possible to discuss specifics and book in for an appointment at his studio (Map p116, B1). Payment can be made in cash or via PayPal.

steamer baskets, long chopsticks meant for stirring pots and pretty ceramic bowls. (上海街; Yau Ma Tei; Ⓜ Yau Ma Tei, exit C)

Tin Hau Temple   TAOIST TEMPLE

4 ⊙ Map p116, C4

This large, incense-filled sanctuary built in the 19th century is one of Hong Kong's most famous Tin Hau (Goddess of the Sea) temples. The public square out front is Yau Ma Tei's communal heart where fishers once laid out their hemp ropes in the sun next to Chinese banyans that today shade chess players and elderly men. (天后廟; ☑ 852 2385 0759; www.ctc.org.hk; cnr Temple & Public Square Sts, Yau Ma Tei; ⊙ 8am-5pm; Ⓜ Yau Ma Tei, exit C)

Wholesale Fruit Market   MARKET

5 ⊙ Map p116, B3

This historic and still operating market, founded in 1913, is a cluster of one- and two-storey brick and stone buildings with pre-WWII signboards. It is a hive of activity from 4am to 6am when fresh fruit is loaded on and off trucks, and bare-backed workers manoeuvre piles of boxes under the moon. The market is bounded by Ferry St, Waterloo Rd and Reclamation St with Shek Lung St running through it. (油麻地果欄; cnr Shek Lung & Reclamation Sts, Yau Ma Tei; ⊙ 2-6am; Ⓜ Yau Ma Tei, exit B2)

STRIPPED PIXEL/SHUTTERSTOCK ©

Tin Hau Temple

Eating

Australia Dairy Company   CAFE $

6 Map p116, B5

Long waits and rude service are the standard at this beloved Hong Kong *cha chaan teng* (tea house), famed for its scrambled egg sandwiches, macaroni and ham soup, and milk pudding. An experience to be had. (澳洲牛奶公司; ☎852 2730 1356; 47-49 Parkes St, Jordan; meals HK$30-50; ☺7.30am-11pm Wed-Mon; Ⓜ Jordan exit C2)

Sun Sin   NOODLES $

7 Map p116, B3

A Michelin-praised brisket shop in a 'hood known for brothels, Sun Sin has kept quality up and prices down despite its laurels. Succulent cuts of meat are served in a broth with radish, in a chunky tomato soup, or as a curry. At peak times, makeshift tables are available upstairs for those who prize food over comfort. (新仙清湯腩; ☎852 2332 6872; 37 Portland St, Yau Ma Tei; meals HK$40-65; ☺11am-midnight; Ⓜ Yau Ma Tei, exit B2)

BBQ Lobster
BARBECUE $

8 Map p116, B5

The most comfortable of three neighbouring branches, this buzzing eatery lures Kowloon gluttons with scrumptious grilled skewers that are 30% to 50% cheaper than the same in Soho. With fresh seven-inch prawns at only HK$17 each and vegetarian options aplenty, indulgence is the norm. In between sticks, cleanse your palate with a sip of Hoegaarden or a zesty white. (龍蝦燒; ☏852 2374 9888; 7 Man Ying St, Ferry Point, Yau Ma Tei; skewers HK$12-35; ◷5pm-3am; ✏; Ⓜ Jordan, exit A)

Good Hope Noodle
NOODLES $

9 Map p116, C2

This 40-year-old shop has retained its Michelin commendation and fan following. Now the al dente egg noodles, bite-sized wontons and silky congee that have won hearts for decades continue to be cooked the old way, but are served in neat, modern surrounds. (好旺角麵家; ☏852 2384 6898; Shop 5-6, 18 Fa Yuen St, Mong Kok; meals HK$30-90; ◷11am-12.45am; Ⓜ Mong Kok, exit D3)

Mido Café
CAFE $

10 Map p116, B4

This retro *cha chaan tang* (tea house; 1950) with mosaic tiles and metal latticework stands astride a street corner that comes to life at sundown. Ascend to the upper floor and take a seat next to a wall of iron-framed windows overlooking Tin Hau Temple – its atmosphere is what makes it Kowloon's most famous tea cafe, despite passable food and service. (美都餐室; ☏852 2384 6402; 63 Temple St, Yau Ma Tei; meals HK$40-90; ◷9am-10pm; Ⓜ Yau Ma Tei, exit B2)

Nathan Congee and Noodle
NOODLES $

11 Map p116, C5

This low-key eatery has been making great congee and noodles for the last half-century. Order a side of fritters

---

Understand
Badass Mah-jong

Shanghai St in Yau Ma Tei is home to a few mah-jong parlours (麻將舘).

In the 1950s, the four-player game of mah-jong was so popular that the British, despite their antigambling policy, began issuing licences to mah-jong parlours. In their heyday, there were over 150; now only a few dozen are left.

Brightly lit and filled with cigarette smoke, mah-jong parlours were often featured in gangster films as they were associated with the triads – the Hong Kong Mafia. Now with the police keeping a close eye, they're little more than the noisy playgrounds of players.

Most of these places have signs reading '麻將娛樂' ('mah-jong entertainment'). You can enter for a peek, but picture-taking is forbidden.

Jewellery for sale at Jade Market

(to be dunked into congee and eaten slightly soggy), tackle a pyramidal rice dumpling, or conquer the blanched fish skin tossed with parsley and peanuts. (彌敦粥麵家; ☑852 2771 4285; 11 Saigon St, Yau Ma Tei; meals HK$60; ⏰7.30am-11.30pm; Ⓜ Jordan, exit B2)

Drinking

Boo
BAR

12 Ⓞ Map p116, C5

This low-key gay bar on Nathan Rd with a karaoke jukebox seems to attract huggable 'bear' types in the local gay community; there's a DJ every Saturday from 9pm. (☑852 2736 6168; 5th fl, Pearl Oriental Tower, 225 Nathan Rd, Jordan; ⏰7pm-2am Sun-Thu, to 4am Fri, 9pm-4am Sat, happy hour 7-9pm; Ⓜ Jordan, exit C1)

Kubrick Bookshop Café
CAFE

13 Ⓞ Map p116, B4

The airy bookshop-cafe attached to the **Broadway Cinematheque** (百老匯電影 中心; ☑852 2388 3188; Ground fl, Prosperous Gardens, 3 Public Square St, Yau Ma Tei; Ⓜ Yau Ma Tei, exit C) serves decent coffee and simple eats, attracting an eclectic, arty crowd. While waiting for your cuppa, you can browse the shop's strong collection of art, film and cultural studies titles. (☑852 2384 8929; www.kubrick.com. hk; Shop H2, Prosperous Garden, 3 Public Square St, Yau Ma Tei; ⏰11.30am-9.30pm; Ⓜ Yau Ma Tei, exit C)

Entertainment

Canton Singing House   LIVE MUSIC

14 ⭐ Map p116, B4

The oldest and most atmospheric of the singalong parlours, Canton resembles a film set with its mirror balls and glowing shrines. Each session features 20 singers, all with fan following. Patrons tip a minimum of HK$20 (per patron) if they like a song. (艷陽天; 49-51 Temple St, Yau Ma Tei; HK$20; ⏰3-7pm & 8pm-5am; Ⓜ Yau Ma Tei, exit C)

Jyut Wan Go Zo   LIVE MUSIC

This long-standing singalong place (see 14 ⭐ Map p116, B4) is large and slightly shabby. For HK$50, you can make a dedication to the singers or sing with them. (粵韻歌座; Yuèyùn Gēzuò; 53-57 Temple St, Yau Ma Tei; HK$20; ⏰3.30-7.30pm & 8pm-4am; Ⓜ Yau Ma Tei, exit C)

Shopping

Chan Wah Kee Cutlery Store   HOMEWARES

15 🔒 Map p116, B5

At this humble shop, octogenarian Mr Chan, one of Asia's few remaining master knife-sharpeners, uses nine different stones to grind each blade, and alternates between water and oil. If you bring him your blade, he charges between HK$100 and HK$600 with a three-month wait.

But if you buy from him, and he has a great selection, he'll do it there and then. (陳華記刀莊; 📞852 2730 4091; 278D Temple St, Yau Ma Tei; ⏰11am-6pm Thu-Tue; Ⓜ Jordan, exit C2)

Shanghai Street   MARKET

Wander Kowloon's kitchen district (see 3 ◎ Map p116, B4) for food-related souvenirs such as wooden mooncake moulds, chopsticks, woks and ceramic teapots. (上海街; Yau Ma Tei; Ⓜ Yau Ma Tei, exit C)

Jade Market   MARKET

16 🔒 Map p116, B4

The covered Jade Market, split into two parts by Battery St, has hundreds of stalls selling all varieties and grades of jade. But unless you really know your nephrite from your jadeite, it's not wise to buy expensive pieces here. Some of the best gets here are not jade at all, but pretty, vintage-y ceramic bead necklaces and bracelets, or coloured wooden beads with double happiness signs. (玉器市場; Battery St & Kansu St, Yau Ma Tei; ⏰10am-6pm; Ⓜ Yau Ma Tei, exit C)

Ladies' Market   MARKET

17 🔒 Map p116, C2

The Tung Choi Street market is a cheek-by-jowl affair offering cheap clothes and trinkets. Vendors start setting up their stalls as early as noon, but it's best to get here between 1pm and 6pm when there's much more on offer. Beware, the sizes stocked here tend to suit

Understand
Hong Kong Occult

Feng Shui

Literally meaning 'wind water', feng shui (or geomancy) aims at maintaining balance among the natural elements to create a harmonious environment. It's been practiced since the 12th century, and continues to influence the design of everything from high-rises to highways in Hong Kong. To disorient evil spirits, which can only travel in a straight line, doors are often positioned at an angle to each other. Ideally, homes and businesses should have a view of calm water – even a fish tank helps.

Fortune Telling

A common method of divination is the use of *chim* – the bamboo 'fortune sticks' found at temples. The process involves shaking a canister filled with these sticks until one falls to the ground, while contemplating a problem to which you need an answer. Each stick bears a numeral corresponding to lines of poetry printed on a slip of paper that's held by the temple guardian. You take the fallen stick to the temple guardian to redeem the paper, then ask a fortune teller to interpret it for you.

the lissom Asian frame. A terrific place to soak up local atmosphere. (通菜街, 女人街; Tung Choi Street Market; Tung Choi St; ⏱noon-11.30pm; Ⓜ Mong Kok, exit D3)

Sino Centre
MALL

19 Map p116, B2

This shabby go-to place for all things related to Asian animation and comics will give you a taste of local culture. Its tiny shops carry new and back issues of Japanese manga, action figures, old-fashioned video games and other kidult bait that attracts a largely male following. (信和中心; 582-592 Nathan Rd, Mong Kok; ⏱10am-10pm; Ⓜ Yau Ma Tei, exit A2)

Yue Hwa Chinese Products Emporium
DEPARTMENT STORE

19 Map p116, C5

This five-storey behemoth is one of the few old-school Chinese department stores left in the city. Gets here include silk scarves, traditional Chinese baby clothes and embroidered slippers, jewellery both cheap and expensive, pretty patterned chopsticks and ceramics, plastic acupuncture models and calligraphy equipment (to name a few). The top floor is all about tea, with various vendors offering free sips. Food is in the basement. (裕華國貨; ☏852 3511 2222; www.yuehwa.com; 301-309 Nathan Rd, Jordan; ⏱10am-10pm; Ⓜ Jordan, exit A)

Top Sights
Sik Sik Yuen Wong Tai Sin Temple

Getting There

The temple is north of Wong Tai Sin MTR station, in the middle of the Wong Tai Sin area.

Ⓜ**MTR** Wong Tai Sin, exit B2

A sensory whirl of roofs and pillars, intricate latticework, bridges, flowers and incense, this Taoist temple, built in 1973, has something for all walks of Hong Kong society, from pensioners and tycoons to office workers and students. Some locals even come to get hitched here – as this is an appointed temple for Taoist weddings.

Wong Tai Sin

The complex is dedicated to a deified healer named Wong Tai Sin who, as a shepherd in Zhèjiāng province, was said to have transformed boulders into sheep. In fact, the whole district is named after him – ironic given he is said to have been a hermit. When he was 15 an immortal taught Wong how to make a herbal potion that could cure all illnesses. He is thus worshipped both by the sick and those trying to avoid illness. The term 'Wong Tai Sin' is also a synonym for someone who's generous to a fault.

Main Altar & Gardens

Taoist ceremonies take place at the main altar. The image of the deity was brought to Hong Kong from Guǎngdōng province in 1915. Behind the altar and to the right are the Good Wish Gardens, replete with pavilions (the hexagonal Unicorn Hall, with carved doors and windows, is the most beautiful), zigzag bridges and carp ponds.

Nearby: Chi Lin Nunnery

Just one MTR stop away from the temple is this arresting Buddhist nunnery (p125), rebuilt completely of wood in 1998 – with not a single nail – in the style of a Tang dynasty monastery. The 3.5-hectare Nan Lian Garden, connected to the nunnery, was built in the style of a Tang dynasty garden, and features a koi pond, Buddhist pines and a pagoda.

嗇色園黃大仙祠

☎ 852 2351 5640, 852 2327 8141

www.siksikyuen.org.hk

2 Chuk Yuen Village, Wong Tai Sin

donation HK$2

🕙 7am-5.30pm

Ⓜ Wong Tai Sin, exit B2

☑ Top Tips

▶ The temple can easily be combined with a trip to **Chi Lin Nunnery** (志蓮淨苑; ☎ 852 2354 1888; www.chilin.org; 5 Chi Lin Dr, Diamond Hill; admission free; 🕙 nunnery 9am-4.30pm, garden 6.30am-7pm; Ⓜ Diamond Hill, exit C2)

✗ Take a Break

▶ Head to Diamond Hill and eat at the **Chi Lin Vegetarian** (志蓮素齋、龍門樓; Long Men Lou; ☎ 852 3658 9388; 60 Fung Tak Rd, Nan Lian Garden; meals from HK$200; 🕙 noon-9pm Mon-Fri, 11.30am-9pm Sat & Sun; 🖊; Ⓜ Diamond Hill, exit C2) restaurant.

▶ Alternatively, head south a kilometre or so to Kowloon City for superb Thai food.

Top Sights
Tian Tan Buddha

Getting There

🚢 **Ferry** Outlying Islands Terminal, Central Pier 6 to Mui Wo, Lantau Island

Ⓜ **MTR** Tung Chung

🚌 **Bus** 2 from Mui Wo, bus 23 from Tung Chung

At 23m (10 storeys), Tian Tan Buddha on Ngong Ping Plateau, Lantau Island, is the world's tallest seated bronze Buddha statue. It can be seen aerially as you fly into Hong Kong, or on a clear day from Macau, but nothing beats coming up close and personal with this much-loved spiritual icon over 500m up in the western hills of Lantau.

'Big Buddha'

Unveiled in 1993, this enormous likeness of Lord Gautama was created by China Aerospace Science and Technology, the designer of China's spaceships.

It's well worth climbing the 268 steps for a closer look at the statue and the surrounding views. The second level of the podium has a tiny exhibition hall with oil paintings and ceramic plaques of the Buddha's life and teachings. The large computerised bell within the Buddha rings 108 times during the day to symbolise escape from the '108 troubles of mankind'. Visitors are requested to observe some decorum in dress and behaviour. It is forbidden to bring meat or alcohol into the grounds.

The Buddha's birthday, a public holiday in April or May, is a lively time to visit when thousands make the pilgrimage.

Po Lin Monastery

Po Lin Monastery, a huge Buddhist complex built in 1924, is more of a tourist honeypot than a religious retreat. Most of the buildings you'll see on arrival are new, with the older, simpler ones tucked away behind them.

Ngong Ping 360

The most spectacular way to get to the plateau is by the 5.7km **Ngong Ping 360** (昂平360纜車; adult/child/concession one way HK$130/65/90, return HK$185/95/130; ☉10am-6pm Mon-Fri, 9am-6.30pm Sat, Sun & public holidays), a cable car linking Ngong Ping with Tung Chung down the hill. The journey over the bay and the mountains takes 25 minutes.

寶蓮禪寺

☎852 2985 5248

Lantau Island

☉9am-6pm

☑ **Top Tips**

▶ Book your cable-car tickets online in advance to avoid some of the wait.

▶ The glass-bottomed Crystal Car is well worth the extra HK$60, plus it has shorter lines.

▶ If the wait for the cable cars is too long, consider taking the bus up and riding the cable car down.

✗ **Take a Break**

▶ The monastery's **Po Lin Vegetarian** (寶蓮禪寺齋堂; ☎852 2985 5248; Ngong Ping; set meals regular/deluxe HK$60/100; ☉11.30am-4.30pm; ✗) restaurant serves meat-free Buddhist cuisine.

▶ To the left of the monastery, a small snack shop sells lovely handmade sweets.

Explore

Trip to Macau

China's Special Administrative Region (SAR) of Macau may be known as the Vegas of the East, but the city has so much more to offer than casinos. It's where fortresses, cathedrals and streets evoking the style of its former Portuguese masters, mingle with Chinese temples and shrines. And, of course, no trip to Macau is complete without enjoying Macanese food, a delicious celebration of hybridism.

The Sights in a Day

Devote two hours to the **Ruins of the Church of St Paul** (p130), its **small museum** (p131), and their neighbour – the **Macau Museum** (p138) in Monte Fort. Wander southwest through the tiny streets towards the Inner Harbour, making stops at the **Mandarin's House** (p137) and **St Joseph's Seminary & Church** (p131). Have lunch at **Clube Militar de Macau** (p139).

After lunch, head north to the charming **St Lazarus Church District** (p137) to browse the boutiques and galleries. Then head up to **Guia Fort** (p136) to see the gorgeous **Chapel of Our Lady of Guia** (p136). Don't miss the lighthouse and the panoramic views of the city. Then, if there's time, pay a visit to the magnificent **Kun Iam Temple** (p138), Macau's oldest temple.

Have dinner at **Antonio** (p139) in Taipa. Return to Macau Peninsula for drinks and live music at **Macau Soul** (p139) or check out **Studio City** (p141).

For a local's day in Macau, see p132.

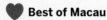

Top Sights

Ruins of the Church of St Paul (p130)

Local Life

Exploring Taipa & Coloane Islands (p132)

Best of Macau

Eating
António (p139)

Clube Militar de Macau (p139)

Cafe Nga Tim (p133)

Drinking
Macau Soul (p139)

Single Origin (p140)

Getting There

⚓ **Ferry** Catch the TurboJet from the Hong Kong–Macau Ferry Terminal or the China Ferry Terminal. Both trips take about an hour.

Top Sights
Ruins of the Church of St Paul

Essentially a magnificent gate to nowhere, the ruins of the Church of St Paul are Macau's most treasured icon. Once part of a Jesuit church, it was designed by an Italian Jesuit and built by exiled Japanese Christians and Chinese craftsmen in 1602. A fire in 1835 wiped out everything except the weathered facade and the majestic stairway. Yet with surviving statues and engravings making up what some call a 'sermon in stone', it's one of the greatest monuments to Christianity in Asia.

大三巴牌坊, Ruinas de Igreja de São Paulo

◉ Map p134, B2

Travessa de São Paulo

admission free

🚍 8A, 17, 26, disembark at Luís de Camões Garden

Asian Details

The facade is full of Asian features. On the third tier, for example, is the Virgin Mary being assumed into heaven along with angels and two flowers: the peony, representing China, and the chrysanthemum, a symbol of Japan. To her right is the apocalyptic woman (Mary) slaying a seven-headed hydra; the Japanese *kanji* reads: 'The holy mother tramples the heads of the dragon'. Bring binoculars if you like history.

Museum & Crypt

This small **museum** (天主教藝術博物館和墓室, Museu de Arte Sacra e Cripta; admission free; ⊙9am-6pm) contains polychrome carved wooden statues, silver chalices and oil paintings, including a copy of a 17th-century painting depicting the crucifixion of Japanese Christians at Nagasaki. The adjoining crypt contains the remains of Asian Christian martyrs and the tomb of Alessandro Valignano, who's credited with establishing Christianity in Japan.

Nearby: Churches

With a scalloped entrance canopy (European), beams and rafters (Chinese) and China's oldest dome, **St Joseph's Seminary & Church** (聖若瑟修院及聖堂, Capela do Seminario Sao Jose; Rua do Seminario; ⊙church 10am-5pm; 🚌9, 16, 18, 28B) is Macau's most beautiful example of tropicalised baroque architecture. The 17th century baroque **Church of St Dominic** (玫瑰堂, Igreja de São Domingos; Largo de São Domingos; ⊙10am-6pm; 🚌3, 6, 26A), in sunny yellow, has a lovely altar and ecclesiastical art in its treasury.

☑ Top Tips

▶ After leaving the crypt, head southeast to see the Macau Museum (p138).

▶ Don't miss the nearby St Lazarus Church District (p137), which features some of the city's most beautiful architecture.

✕ Take a Break

▶ Have a cocktail and possibly catch some music at nearby Macau Soul (p139).

Local Life
Exploring Taipa & Coloane Islands

Taipa was created from two islands joined together by silt from the Pearl River. Land reclamation has succeeded in doing the same thing to Taipa and Coloane, now joined by the Cotai Strip, Cotai being a portmanteau of Coloane and Taipa. Taipa has rapidly urbanised, though you'll still find traditional shops alongside charming Macanese bistros. The small island of Coloane was once a haven for pirates but today largely retains Macau's old way of life.

....

❶ **Taipa Village**
Take bus 22, 26 or 33 to get to this village in the south of the island, where the historical part of Taipa is best preserved. With a tidy sprawl of traditional Chinese shops and some excellent restaurants, the village is punctuated by grand colonial villas,

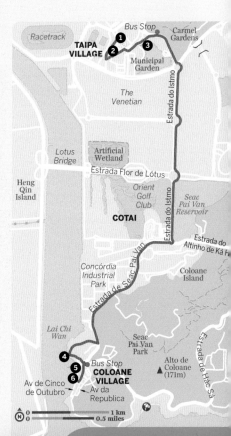

churches and ancient temples. Avenida da Praia, a tree-lined esplanade with wrought-iron benches, is perfect for a leisurely stroll.

② Pak Tai Temple

Pak Tai Temple (Rua do Regedor; 🚌 22, 28A, 26) sits quietly in a breezy square framed by old trees. It is dedicated to a martial deity – the Taoist God (*Tai*) of the North (*Pak*) – who defeated the Demon King who was terrorising the universe. A pair of Chinese lions guards the entrance to the temple. On the third day of the third lunar month, Cantonese opera performances take place here.

③ Taipa Houses-Museum

Further afield, the pastel-toned **villas** (龍環葡韻住宅式博物館, Casa Museum da Taipa; 📞 853 2882 7103; Avenida da Praia, Carmo Zone, Taipa village; adult/student MOP$5/2, child & senior free, Sun free; 🕙 10am-5.30pm Tue-Sun; 🚌 11, 15, 22, 28A, 30, 33, 34) here were once the summer residences of middle-class Macanese; now they're museums showcasing Portuguese traditions and local life in the early 20th century.

④ Coloane's Stilt Houses

Head to Coloane by bus 21A from the bus stop on Estrada Governador Nobrede Carvalho, and alight at Coloane Village. In **Rua Dos Navegantes**, Coloane's old fishing village, there are a few stilt houses of colourful corrugated metal, that were once landing spots for houseboats. You'll see them near **Largo do Cais**, the square just off the old pier of Coloane. From the square, take the slope to the right of the Servicos de Alfangega building. After two minutes, you'll see the cavernous cadaver of a shipyard, also on stilts.

⑤ Chapel of St Francis Xavier

One of Coloane's highlights is this eccentric **chapel** (聖方濟各教堂, Capela de São Francisco Xavier; Rua do Caetano, Largo Eduardo Marques, Coloane; 🕙 10am-8pm; 🚌 15, 21A, 25, 26A), built in 1928, which contains paintings of the infant Christ with a Chinese Madonna, and other artefacts that illustrate how Christianity and colonialism were intertwined.

⑥ Chinese-Portuguese Fare & Egg Tarts

Finish your walk with a Chinese-Portuguese meal at nearby **Café Nga Tim** (雅憩花園餐廳; Rua do Caetano, Coloane village; mains MOP$70-200; 🕙 noon-1am; 🚻; 🚌 21A, 25, 26A). Enjoy the small-town atmosphere and, possibly, banter with the friendly owner – a guitar- and erhu-strumming ex-policeman named Feeling Wong. Before hopping on the bus back to Macau Peninsula, grab a couple of *pastéis de nata* (warm egg-custard tarts) from **Lord Stow's Bakery** (澳門安德魯餅店; 1 Rua da Tassara; egg tarts MOP$9; 🕙 7am-10pm Thu-Tue, to 7pm Wed).

SOUTH CHINA SEA

Ponte da Amizade Friendship Bridge

Av Norte da Amizade

Outer Harbour Ferry Terminal

Fisherman's Wharf

4 Macau Museum of Art

Avenida Xian Xing Hai

Av Dr Sun Yat Sen

NAPE

Rua dos Pescadores

Cemetery Reservoir

Av do Conselheiro Ferreira de Almeida

7 Kun Iam Temple

Av do Coronel Mesquita

14

9 Red Market

Av Horta e Costa

Rua da Ribeira do Patane

Rotunda de Carlos da Maia

Luís de Camões Garden & Grotto

Lou Lim Ioc Garden

Guia Fortress & Guia Chapel **1**

Guia Hill

Avenida da Luís Gonzaga Gomes

Av do Rodrigo

Tap Seac Square

2 13

St Lazarus Church District

Avenida de Lisboa

Rua de Paris

Jardim des Artes

Ponte Governador Nobre de Carvalho

6

10

Ruins of the Church of St Paul

Estrada do Cemitério

8

Macau Museum

16

Travessa de São Paulo

12

Rua do Almirante Sérgio

Av de Almeida Ribeiro

Rua Central

3 Leal Senado

Largo de St Agostinho

Rua de St

Baía da Praia (Lagos de Nam Van)

Avenida Doutor Stanley Ho

Inner Harbour

Quanshan Waterway

Mandarin's House

5

Penha Hill

Lago Sai Van

Av Dr Sun Yat Sen

Rua da Barra

Rua de São Tiago da Barra

Av da República

Penha

United Chinese Cemetery

Estrada de Pac On

Taipa Grande (160m) ▲

Cemetery

Pak On Bay

Cemetery

Cemetery

Taipa Island

Avenida Dr Sun Yat Sen

Rua de Seng Tou

Rua de Kwong Tung

TAIPA CITY

TAIPA VILLAGE

Carmel Gardens

Municipal Garden

17

Rua Correia da Silva

11

Largo des Bombeiros

Rua do Regedor

Estrada da Baía de N Senhora da Esperança

15 ⚽

Estrada Lou Lim Ieok

Taipa Pequena (111m) ▲

Racetrack

Macau-Taipa Bridge

Sai Van Bridge

For reviews see

◉ Top Sights   p130
⊙ Sights   p136
⊗ Eating   p139
🍸 Drinking   p139
🎭 Entertainment   p141
🛍 Shopping   p141

0   1 km
0   0.5 miles

N

5

6

7

8

A   B   C   D   E

Sights

Guia Fortress & Guia Chapel

FORT, CHURCH

1 Map p134, C2

As the highest point on the peninsula, Guia Fort affords panoramic
views of the city and, when the air
is clear, across to the islands and
China. At the top is the stunning
Chapel of Our Lady of Guia, built in
1622 and retaining almost 100% of
its original features, including some
of Asia's most important frescoes.
Next to it stands the oldest modern
lighthouse on the China coast (1865)
– an attractive 15m-tall structure that
is closed to the public. (東望洋炮台
及聖母雪地殿聖堂, Fortaleza da Guia e
Capela de Guia; admission free; ⏰fortress
6am-6pm, chapel 10am-5.30pm; 🚌2, 2A,
6A, 12, 17, 18, Flora Garden stop)

Tap Seac Square

SQUARE

2 Map p134, C2

This beautiful square surrounded by
important historic buildings from
the 1920s (Cultural Affairs Bureau,
Tap Seac Health Centre, Central Library, Library for Macau's Historical
Archives, **Tap Seac Gallery** (塔石藝文
舘, Galeria Tap Seac; www.macauart.net/ts;
95 Avenida Conselheiro Ferreira de Almeida;
⏰10am-9pm; 🚌)) was designed by
Macanese architect Carlos Marreiros. Marreiros also created the Tap
Seac Health Centre, a contemporary
interpretation of Macau's neoclassi-

cal buildings. (塔石廣場, Praca do Tap
Seac; 🚌7, 8)

Leal Senado

HISTORIC BUILDING

3 Map p134, B2

Facing Largo do Senado is Macau's
most important historical building, the 18th-century 'Loyal Senate',
which houses the Instituto para
os Assuntos Cívicos e Municipais
(IACM; Civic and Municipal Affairs
Bureau). It is so-named because the
body sitting here refused to recognise Spain's sovereignty during the
60 years that it occupied Portugal. In
1654, a dozen years after Portuguese
sovereignty was re-established, King
João IV ordered a heraldic inscrip-
tion to be placed inside the entrance
hall, which can still be seen today.
(民政總署大樓; ☎853 2857 2233; 163
Avenida de Almeida Ribeiro; ⏰9am-9pm
Tue-Sun; 🚌3, 6, 26A, 18A, 33, disembark at
Almeida Ribeiro)

Macau Museum of Art

MUSEUM

4 Map p134, D3

This excellent five-storey museum
has well-curated displays of art created in Macau and China, including
paintings by Western artists like
George Chinnery, who lived in the en-
clave. Other highlights are ceramics
and stoneware excavated in Macau,
Ming- and Qing-dynasty calligraphy
from Guǎngdōng, ceramic statues
from Shíwān (Guǎngdōng) and seal
carvings. The museum also features

COLOURS IN MY LIFE / SHUTTERSTOCK ©

Guia Lighthouse, Fortress and Chapel

19th-century Western historical paintings from all over Asia, and contemporary Macanese art. (澳門藝術博物館, Museu de Arte de Macau; ☏ 853 8791 9814; www.mam.gov.mo; Macau Cultural Centre, Avenida Xian Xing Hai; adult/child MOP$5/2, Sun free; ⏲10am-6.30pm Tue-Sun; ☐1A, 8, 12, 23)

Mandarin's House   HISTORIC BUILDING

5 ◎ Map p134, A3

Built around 1869, the Mandarin's House, with over 60 rooms, was the ancestral home of Zheng Guanying, an influential author-merchant whose readers included emperors, Dr Sun Yatsen and Chairman Mao. The compound features a moon gate, tranquil courtyards, exquisite rooms and a main hall with French windows, all arranged in that labyrinthine style typical of certain Chinese period buildings. There are guided tours in Cantonese on week-end afternoons. (鄭家大屋, Caso do Mandarim; ☏ 853 2896 8820; www.wh.mo/mandarinhouse; 10 Travessa de Antonio da Silva; admission free; ⏲10am-5.30pm Thu-Tue; ☐28B, 18)

St Lazarus Church District   AREA

6 ◎ Map p134, B2

A lovely neighbourhood with colonial-style houses and cobbled streets makes for some of Macau's

Mandarin's House (p137)

best photo-ops. Designers and other creative types like to gather here, setting up shop and organising artsy events. (瘋堂斜巷, Calcada da Igreja de Sao Lazaro; www.cipa.org.mo; 🚌 7, 8)

Kun Iam Temple
BUDDHIST TEMPLE

 7 🎯 Map p134, C1

Macau's oldest temple was founded in the 13th century, but the present structures date back to 1627. Its roofs are embellished with porcelain figurines and its halls are lavishly decorated. Inside the main one stands the likeness of Kun Iam, the Goddess of Mercy; to the left of the altar is a statue of a bearded *arhat* rumoured to represent Marco Polo. The first

Sino-American treaty was signed at a round stone table in the temple's terraced gardens in 1844. (觀音廟, Templo de Kun Iam; 2 Avenida do Coronel Mesquita; ⏰ 7am-5.30pm; 🚌 1A, 10, 18A, stop Travessa de Venceslau de Morais)

Macau Museum
MUSEUM

8 🎯 Map p134, B2

This interesting museum inside Monte Fort will give you a taste of Macau's history. The 1st floor introduces the territory's early history and includes an elaborate section on Macau's religions. Highlights of the 2nd floor include a recreated firecracker factory and a recorded reading in the local dialect by Macanese poet José dos

Santos Ferreira (1919–93). The top floor focuses on new architecture and urban-development plans. (澳門博物館 | Museu de Macau; ☎853 2835 7911; www.macaumuseum.gov.mo; 112 Praceta do Museu de Macau; admission MOP$15, 15th of month free; ⊙10am-5.30pm Tue-Sun; ☐7, 8, disembark at Social Welfare Bureau)

Red Market
MARKET

9 ◉ Map p134 , B1

Designed by Macanese architect Júlio Alberto Basto, this three-storey art-deco building with a clocktower houses a lively wet market. It was so-named because of the red bricks used in its construction. (紅街市大樓, Mercado Almirante Lacerda; cnr Avenida do Almirante Lacerda & Avenida Horta e Costa; ⊙7.30am-7.30pm; ☐23, 32)

Eating

Clube Militar de Macau
PORTUGUESE $$

10 Map p134, B3

Housed in a distinguished colonial building, with fans spinning lazily above, the Military Club takes you back in time to a slower and quieter Macau. The simple and delicious Portuguese fare is complemented by an excellent selection of wine and cheese from Portugal. The MOP$153 buffet is excellent value. Reservations are required for dinner and weekend lunches. (陸軍俱樂部; ☎853

2871 4000; 975 Avenida da Praia Grande; meals MOP$150-400; ⊙1.45-2.30pm & 7-10.30pm Mon-Fri, noon-2.30pm & 7-10pm Sat & Sun; ☐6, 28C)

António
PORTUGUESE $$$

11 ✗ Map p134, D8

The cosy mahogany-framed dining room, the meticulously thought-out menu and the entertaining chef, António Coelho, all make this the go-to place for traditional Portuguese food. If you can only try one Portuguese restaurant in Macau, make it this one. The octopus salad, home-made sausage (served flaming) and the African chicken are exceptional. (安東尼奧; ☎853 2888 8668; www.antoniomacau.com; 7 Rua dos Clérigos, Taipa village; meals MOP$350-1200; ⊙noon-midnight; ☐22, 26)

Drinking

Macau Soul
BAR

12 ⬚ Map p134, B2

An elegant haven in wood and stained glass, where twice a month a jazz band plays to a packed audience. On most nights, though, Thelonious Monk fills the air as customers chat with the owners and dither over their 430 Portuguese wines. Opening hours vary; phone ahead. (澳感廊; ☎853 2836 5182; www.macausoul.com; 31a Rua de São Paulo; ⊙3-10pm Wed & Thu, to midnight Fri-Sun; ☐8A, 17, 26)

GUOZHONGHUA/SHUTTERSTOCK ©

Studio City

Single Origin

COFFEE

13 Map p134, C2

This airy corner cafe opened by coffee professional Keith Fong makes a mean shot of espresso. You can choose your poison from a daily selection of 10 beans from various regions. If you can't decide, the well-trained barristas are more than happy to help. (單品; ☏853 6698 7475; 19 Rua de Abreu Nunes; coffee MOP$35; ⏱11.30am-8pm Mon-Sat, 2-7pm Sun; 🛜; 🚌2, 4, 7, 7A, 8)

Lung Wah Tea House

CANTONESE **$**

14 Map p134, C1

There's grace in the retro furniture and the casual way it's thrown together in this airy Cantonese teahouse (c 1963). Take a booth by the windows overlooking the Red Market, where the teahouse buys its produce every day. There's no English menu; just point and take. Lung Wah sells a fine array of Chinese teas. (龍華茶樓; ☏853 2857 4456; 3 Rua Norte do Mercado Aim-Lacerda; dim sum from MOP$14, tea MOP$10, meals MOP$50-180; ⏱7am-2pm; 🚻; 🚌23, 32)

Entertainment

Studio City CASINO

15 ⭐ Map p134, E8

You can recognise this new casino from afar by the figure-8-shaped 'Golden Reel' at its centre, a double Ferris wheel with views across the Cotai Strip. This Hollywood-themed casino complex is one of Macau's more family-friendly, with a Warner Brothers–themed indoor kiddie amusement park and a (very entertaining) Batman flight-simulation ride (MOP$150). Beyond the fully loaded casino, you'll find a 1600-room hotel, a mall, a house magic show and a food court designed to look like old Macau. (☎853 8865 8888; www.studiocity-macau.com; Estrada Flor de Lotus, Cotai; 🚻; 🚌25, 26A)

Shopping

Livraria Portuguesa BOOKS, GIFTS

16 🔒 Map p134, B2

Right in the heart of Macau's historic district, this two-storey bookshop carries both English and Portuguese titles, including some hard-to-find Macanese cookbooks. It also stocks gift items, like imported Portuguese soaps and perfumes. Founded more than 30 years ago, it's one of the few places in Macau where you can reliably hear Portuguese spoken. (Portuguese Bookstore; ☎853 2851 5915; Rua do São Domingos 18; ◷11am-7pm; 🚌3, 4, 6A, 8A, 19, 33)

Cunha Bazaar GIFTS & SOUVENIRS

17 🔒 Map p134, D8

This four-storey shop on the corner of Taipa village's Rua do Cunha pedestrian street has the motherlode of made-in-Macau gifts, T-shirts, candies and more. You'll find traditional foods like almond cookies and jerky on the ground floor, while the 1st floor is dedicated to goods bearing the image of Macau's own Soda Panda, a perpetually grumpy cartoon panda who likes to do Macanese things like eat egg tarts and play roulette. The remaining two floors are dedicated to leather goods, ceramics, notebooks, sketches and so on by local designers. (www.cunhabazaar.com; Rua do Cunha 33-35, Taipa village; ◷9.30am-10pm)

The Best of
Hong Kong

Hong Kong's Best Walks

Hong Kong's Best...

Junk tour of Hong Kong harbour (p159)
IAKOV KALININ/GETTY IMAGES ©

Best Walks
Hong Kong's Wholesale District

🏃 The Walk

Sheung Wan became a trading hub in the mid-19th century, when turmoil in China caused Chinese business men to flee to Hong Kong. They set up businesses in Sheung Wan, trading in dried seafood, herbs and rice. As more migrants came, the area around Tai Ping Shan St became the heart of the Chinese community, with its own temples and funeral parlours. Sheung Wan was also tied to Dr Sun Yat-sen, who went to school here and, later, held secret meetings in the area as a revolutionary.

Start Tram Kennedy Town, Sutherland St stop,

Finish Ⓜ Sheung Wan, exit B

Length 1.9km; one hour

🍴 Take a Break

Mrs Pound (p35)

CLAUDIO ZACCHERINI/SHUTTERSTOCK ©

Dried seafood shops at Sheung Wan market

❶ Dried Seafood Shops

From the Sutherland St stop of the Kennedy Town tram, have a look at (and a sniff of) Des Voeux Rd West's many dried seafood shops, piled with all manner of desiccated sea life: scallops, abalone, sea cucumbers, oysters, conch and fish maw.

❷ Herbal Medicine Traders

Head south on Ko Shing St to browse the positively medieval-sounding goods on offer from the herbal medicine traders. At the end of Ko Shing St, re-enter Des Voeux Rd West and walk northeast. Continue along Connaught Rd Central, where you'll pass the Edwardian building housing the **Western Market**.

❸ Ginseng & Bird's Nest Shops

At the corner of Morrison St, walk south to Wing Lok St and Bonham Strand, which are both lined with shops selling ginseng and edible bird's nests, the latter made from the salivary excretions of cave swifts, and consumed (as a sweet soup) for their proven ability to regenerate human cells.

4 Tai Ping Shan Temples

Turn right onto Queen's Rd Central and passby shops selling paper funeral offerings for the dead. Climb up Possession St, then take a right into Hollywood Rd, a left into Po Yan Stand then a left into Tai Ping Shan

St, where you'll spot three temples. Look to the right for **Pak Sing Ancestral Hall** (p32) and **Kwun Yum Temple**, and to the left for **Tai Sui Temple**.

5 Antique Shops

Follow Upper Station St to the start of Hollywood Rd's antique shops. There's a vast choice of curios, replicas and a few rare, mostly Chinese, treasures.

6 Man Mo Temple

Continuing east on Hollywood Rd brings you to **Man Mo Temple** (p28), one of the oldest temples in the territory and dedicated to the civil and martial gods Man Cheung and Kwan Yu. From here catch bus 26 or head north towards the harbour for Sheung Wan MTR station on Des Voeux Rd.

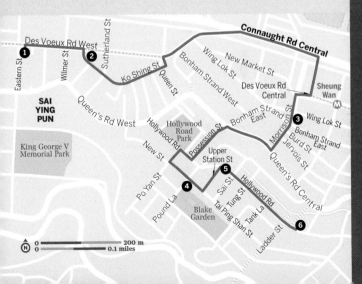

Best Walks
Wan Chai's Forgotten Streets

🏃 The Walk

Wan Chai's coastline used to run near the tram tracks on Johnston Rd before zealous land reclamation pushed the shoreline to the north. During that time, the area around Queen's Rd East and Johnston Rd was a fishing village with shrines and temples overlooking the sea. After the British came, shipyards were built along the bay and 'second-rank' Europeans who could not afford to live on Victoria Peak made their homes on the hills south of Queen's Rd East. Though new Wan Chai is an exciting commercial district with skyscrapers and five-star hotels, for those keen on exploration, the south side of the (tram) tracks will always be more interesting.

Start Pak Tai Temple Ⓜ Wan Chai, exit A3

Finish Star St Ⓜ Admiralty, exit F

Length 1.2km; two hours

🍴 Take a Break
Stone Nullah Tavern (p77)

PSGXXX/SHUTTERSTOCK ©

Blue House (p70)

❶ Pak Tai Temple

A five-minute stroll south of Wan Chai MTR station, past Johnston Rd, lies stunning **Pak Tai Temple** (p70), built 150 years ago by local residents.

❷ Blue House

Further down the slope on Stone Nullah Lane, the **Blue House** (p70) will show you what life was like in Wan Chai in the last century (it has no toilet-flushing facilities). The Blue House was painted its current colour during a renovation in the 1920s because the government had surplus blue paint.

❸ Old Wan Chai Post Office

Head west on Queen's Rd East and glance across at the Streamline Moderne facade of a shopping centre that used to be the Wan Chai Market. Once the neighbourhood hub, the market was used as a mortuary by Japanese forces in WWII. The colonial-style Old Wan Chai Post Office at 221 Queen's Rd East is Hong Kong's oldest (1913).

❹ Spring Garden Lane

Cross the road to take a look at Spring Garden Lane, one of the first areas developed by the British. A British merchant had a lavish residence here named Spring Gardens, and Spring Garden Lane was the length between its north and south gates. In the 1900s the lane harboured many brothels.

❺ Ghost House

Return to the southern side of Queen's Rd East. Peep inside mysterious **Hung Shing Temple** (p70), once a seaside shrine. Just west of the temple turn up the hill along Ship St and stand before the now-derelict **Ghost House** at 55 Nam Koo Terrace. Its history is a wretched one: it was used by Japanese soldiers as a brothel housing 'comfort women' in WWII.

❻ Star Street

The Star St neighbourhood is a quiet corner of Wan Chai, where the old, such as a family-run *dai pai dong* (hawker-style food stall) on St Francis St, exist alongside the new, like hipster boutiques and cafes. On 31 Wing Fung St is a six-storey balconied building in art deco style. Admiralty MTR can be reached by an escalator and underground travelator, entered at the bottom of Wing Fung St.

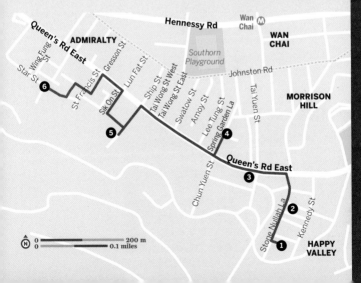

Best Walks
Tsim Sha Tsui

In early colonial days, Tsim Sha Tsui (TST) was a garden city inhabited by Europeans. Nathan Rd was lined by colonial houses and Chinese banyans were planted to provide shade. Chinese people weren't allowed to live in TST until the early 20th century when the area was being developed into a trade hub. After the communist takeover in 1949, many Shanghainese businessmen fled to Hong Kong; some settled in TST. In the northern part of the district are postwar buildings that were once homes to this Chinese ethnic group.

Start Former Kowloon British School; Ⓜ Tsim Sha Tsui, exit B1

Finish Jordan Path; Ⓜ Jordan, exit A

Length 2.5km; two hours

✕ Take a Break
Chicken HOF & Soju Korean (p105)

JANE SWEENEY/GETTY IMAGES ©

Rosary Church (p102)

❶ Former British School

To reach this former **school** (p101), turn right from exit B1 of Tsim Sha Tsui MTR station and walk north along Nathan Rd. Next door is **St Andrew's Anglican Church** (p101), Kowloon's oldest Anglican church. Further north on Nathan Rd, turn right into Austin Rd, a former stronghold of Shanghainese migrants.

❷ Pak On Building

Explore Pak On Building (百安大廈) between Austin Rd and Tak Shing St, with its lobby arcade littered with shops. Down near Tak Shing St there is a liquor store, run by a sweet old couple, that stocks absinthe. Return to Austin Rd. Half way to the fork where Austin Rd branches out into Austin Ave, you'll see the lawns of the Kowloon Green Bowling Club, a gem from colonial times.

❸ Carnival Mansion

Carnival Mansion (嘉華大廈), at 15 Austin

Ave, has a courtyard where you can stare up at a vortex of rickety postwar homes. Inside the buildings are yellow terrazzo staircases with green balustrades made by Shanghainese craftsmen 50 years ago.

❹ Triangular Toilet

Outside Carnival Mansion, you'll spot the curious '**triangular public toilet**' (三角公廁) as it is known to cab drivers. The facility doubles up as a small power station. Continue down Austin Ave and make a left on Chatham Rd South. **Rosary Church** (p102), Kowloon's oldest Catholic church, stands next to **St Mary's Canossian College** (嘉諾撒聖瑪利書院), built in 1900.

❺ Gun Club Hill Barracks

At the big junction, make a left into Austin Rd. The cannon-guarded gates of **Gun Club Hill Barracks** (槍會山軍營), now home to the People's Liberation Army (PLA), is on its other side. Turn into the leafy alley (Jordan Path) right next to the gates.

❻ Jordan Path

As you walk, note how functional buildings (belonging to the PLA) loom up on your right, while the manicured lawns of the colonial recreation clubs unfurl on your left. Just before Jordan Rd, you'll see the **PLA Hospital** (解放軍駐軍醫院) with its darkened windows. Crossing Cox's Rd takes you to the Victorian-style Anglican **Kowloon Union Church**. Continue along Jordan Rd for Jordan MTR station.

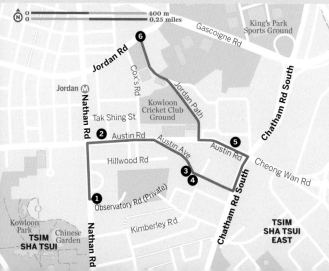

Best
Views

Best Eye-Level Views

Star Ferry Aboard the historic ferry is the best way to view Hong Kong's famous harbour (p176)

Central-Mid-Levels Escalator Turns Soho and Sheung Wan into a moveable feast. (p49)

Trams Sit back and let the city unfold like a carousel of images. (p39)

Happy Valley Racecourse Between mountains and high-rises, the ponies gallop under bright lights at night. (p62)

Aberdeen Promenade Fishing boats and pleasure vessels streak the waters of the typhoon shelter loved by Hollywood. (p87)

Best Vantage Points

Tsim Sha Tsui East Promenade Face to face with Hong Kong's most iconic view. (p96)

Hong Kong Monetary Authority Information Centre Sweeping 55th floor vistas by the edge of Victoria Harbour. (p35)

Bank of China Tower Views stretch all the way to Kowloon Peninsula from the 42nd floor. (p32)

Best Views from a Park

Victoria Peak Revisit Hong Kong Island and Kowloon in the distance, from top down. (p42)

Hong Kong Park Dramatic juxtaposition of skyscrapers and mountains that's uniquely Hong Kong. (p64)

Ocean Park Two rows of cable cars swing between the hill and the South China Sea. (p87)

Best Views from a Bar

Sevva So close to the HSBC Building, it's down-right dizzying. (p38)

MARIA SWARD/GETTY IMAGES ©

InterContinental Lobby Lounge Similar to the Tsim Sha Tsui East Promenade, but with air-con. (p109)

Aqua Spirit A dramatic take on the Island sky-line, especially at night. (p108)

Best Hill-Top Views

Tian Tan Buddha Let Lantau Island unfurl before you from 523m above the sea. (p126)

Signal Hill Garden Pretty views of the harbour from the top of a knoll in Tsim Sha Tsui. (p102)

Guia Fort Skyline decked by casinos and colonial buildings from the highest point on the Macau Peninsula. (p136)

Best
Temples

Most Historically Important

Man Mo Temple Once a court of arbitration for the Chinese who mistrusted British law courts. (p28)

Hung Shing Temple (Wan Chai) Dedicated to the God of Seafarers and sitting on a boulder. (p70)

Hung Shing Temple (Ap Lei Chau) A harbour-facing temple built by fishermen in the 18th century. (p88)

Pak Sing Ancestral Hall Doubled as a clinic and a public ancestral hall for the poor. (p32)

Kun Iam Temple This Buddhist temple in Macau witnessed the signing of an important treaty in 1844. (p138)

Best Non-Taoist Temples

Khalsa Diwan Sikh Temple The city's largest Sikh temple welcomes believers and non-believers. (p67)

Chi Lin Nunnery Immaculate faux-Tang dynasty architecture and Buddhist-style gardens to go with it. (p125)

Po Lin Monastery It's worthwhile paying a visit to Lantau Island to see the Big Buddha. (p127)

Kun Iam Temple Beautiful ceramic figurines and lavish decor at this Buddhist temple in Macau. (p138)

Best Urban Temples

Tin Hau Temple A humble-looking temple complex in Yau Ma Tei's leafy public square. (p118)

Hung Shing Temple (Wan Chai) Dark, mysterious, overlooks a busy road. (p70)

Man Mo Temple Hong Kong's most famous temple sits between Central and Sheung Wan. (p28)

Pak Tai Temple This majestic structure in Wan Chai houses formidable statues of deities. (p70)

HATCHAPONG PALURTCHAIVONG/SHUTTERSTOCK ©

Fook Tak Ancient Temple This tiny, smoke-choked former shrine is Tsim Sha Tsui's only temple. (p101)

Temples with the Most Visual Impact

Sik Sik Yuen Wong Tai Sin Temple Noisy, colourful, flamboyant, and surrounded by high-rises (p124)

Man Mo Temple Incense coils hang from the ceiling like inverted mushrooms. (p28)

Tian Tan Buddha The world's tallest seated outdoor bronze Buddha can be seen from the plane. (p126)

Kun Iam Temple Beautiful ceramic figurines on the roof and ornate decorations in the halls. (p138)

Best
Architecture

Over the centuries Hong Kong has played host to everything, from Taoist temples and Qing dynasty forts to Victorian churches and Edwardian hotels. Until recently, the city's ceaseless cycle of deconstruction and reconstruction meant that the charmingly old were often eagerly replaced by modern marvels. Now, restoration and revitalisation of old buildings of some architectural interest are expected by the public, even if such practices are still far from the norm.

Traditional Chinese

About the only examples of precolonial Chinese architecture left in urban Hong Kong are Tin Hau temples and the Hung Shing temples that date from the early to mid-19th century, including those at Yau Ma Tei, Wan Chai and Ap Lei Chau. For anything more substantial, go to the New Territories to see walled villages, fortresses and ancient pagodas.

Colonial Architecture

Most of what is left of colonial architecture is on Hong Kong Island, especially in Central, though Tsim Sha Tsui on the Kowloon Peninsula is also home to quite a few examples. Many of Hong Kong and Macau's colonial architecture features adaptations for the tropical climate, such as typhoon-resistant roof tiles, just as some Chinese buildings have Western-style motifs.

Modern Architecture

Enthusiasts of modern architecture will have a field day in Hong Kong. Central and Wan Chai are wonderful showcases for modern and contemporary buildings – many designed by internationally celebrated architects.

☑ **Top Tips**

▶ For a list of historic structures, visit the website of the **Hong Kong Antiquities & Monuments Office** (☏ 852 2721 2326; www.amo.gov. hk; 136 Nathan Rd, Tsim Sha Tsui; ⏰ 9am-5pm Mon-Sat; Ⓜ Tsim Sha Tsui, exit A2). Or visit in person: it's inside the Former Kowloon British School (p101) in Tsim Sha Tsui.

▶ For the latest on Hong Kong's preservation efforts, see www.heritage. gov.hk.

Best 18th- & 19th-Century Chinese Buildings

Tin Hau Temple The green-roofed complex that gave Temple Street its name. (p118)

Man Mo Temple Hong Kong's best known temple was founded in Sheung Wan by Chinese merchants. (p28)

Hung Shing Temple (Ap Lei Chau) A structure built by fishermen, that worships the God of Seafarers. (p88)

Pak Sing Ancestral Hall This temple was once clinic, morgue, and public ancestral hall. (p32)

Kun Iam Temple Macau's richly decorated Buddhist temple was where an important treaty was signed. (p138)

Best Colonial Structures

Central Police Station Featuring prison, magistracy and police station, in late-Victorian and other styles. (p49)

Former Marine Police Headquarters One of the oldest (c 1884) and handsomest government buildings still around. (p99)

Clock Tower The only remaining structure of the old Kowloon–Canton Railway is right by the harbour. (p25)

Blackhead Point Tower A charming Edwardian tower that was used to help ships tell the time. (p102)

Former Victoria Barracks Beautifully transformed into the facilities of the Asia Society. (p71)

Flagstaff House The oldest (1846) colonial building in Hong Kong still occupying its original spot. (p65)

St John's Cathedral Victorian Gothic, with stained-glass windows showing scenes of vernacular Hong Kong life. (p35)

Ruins of the Church of St Paul Stately facade in a Southern European style, Asian details. (pictured top left, p130)

Béthanie The fine example of French colonial architecture was a sanatorium for priests. (p88)

Best Fusion Architecture

Ruins of the Church of St Paul Sixteenth-century ruins in Macau. Southern European with Asian details. (p130)

Mandarin's House A graceful Chinese residence in Macau, featuring French windows and other European elements. (p137)

Best Contemporary Buildings

HSBC Building Masterpiece in late modern, high-tech style by Norman Foster. (p26)

Bank of China Tower An awe-inspiring tower of cubes designed by IM Pei. (p32)

Tap Seac Square A gorgeous contemporary interpretation of Macau's neoclassical Southern-European-style buildings. (p136)

Best
Museums & Galleries

Best Collections

Hong Kong Museum of Art Modern and contemporary Hong Kong art, and ancient Chinese art. (p97)

Hong Kong Museum of History Tells the history of Hong Kong via colourful displays. (p99)

Macau Museum of Art Excellent works by Macau's Chinese, Macanese and Western artists, and Shiwan ceramics. (p136)

Liangyi Museum Extraordinary collection of classical Chinese furniture and Eastern-inspired European vanities. (p33)

Blindspot Gallery Specialising in showing the works of Hong Kong's excellent photographers. (p89)

Best Buyable Art

Grotto Fine Art One of very few galleries with a focus on top Hong Kong art. (p58)

Best 'People's' Art Spaces

C&G Artpartment A socially-minded art space in the middle of Mong Kok. (p117)

Most Entertaining

Comix Home Base Fascinating introduction to Hong Kong's comic-book history in a light-flooded historic complex. (p71)

Flagstaff House Museum of Tea Ware Lovely bowls, brewing trays, sniffing cups and teapots. (p65)

Hong Kong Science Museum From gravity to tadpoles, all worldly phenomena explained. (p103)

Hong Kong Space Museum Try 'moonwalking' and eating astronaut ice cream. (p103)

Hong Kong Museum of History Interactive displays and life-sized replicas, especially the 'Hong Kong Story' gallery. (p99)

LONELY PLANET/GETTY IMAGES ©

► **Hong Kong Art Walk** (www.hongkongartwalk.com; ☺Mar) features over 60 galleries on Hong Kong Island opening their doors to visitors and entertaining with food and wine for one night in March.

► **Art Basel Hong Kong** (p78) in May sees hundreds of galleries and dealers from the world over participating to attract potential buyers and art collectors.

Best
Parks & Gardens

Best for Human-Made Beauty

Victoria Peak Garden
Restored 'Victorian' garden of a former governor's summer lodge. (p42)

Hong Kong Park
Artificial waterfalls and ponds with real waterfowl – perfect for wedding photos. (p64)

Nan Lian Garden
Faux Tang-dynasty architecture and gardens decked out with Buddhist pines. (p125)

Most Secluded

Victoria Peak Garden
To reach this peaceful spot, you'll need to make the ascent to Victoria Peak. (p42)

Signal Hill Garden
Possibly the quietest corner of good old Tsim Sha Tsui. (p102)

Nan Lian Garden
A pleasant garden with pagodas and Buddhist pines; connected to Chi Lin Nunnery. (pictured top right; p125)

Middle Road Children's Playground On weekdays, only old folks and migrant workers come here. (p102)

Best for a Picnic

Victoria Peak Garden
Tea-party in style at this faux-Victorian garden with gazebos. (p42)

Victoria Park No shortage of plush blades where you can soak up the sun. (p72)

Kowloon Park Take your pick from lawn, bench or concrete at this former barracks. (p100)

Best for People-Watching

Middle Road Children's Playground Breezy park frequented by all ages and ethnicities. (p102)

Kowloon Park
Locals come to chat, picnic, swim, jog and practise kung fu. (p100)

Victoria Park Hang-out of Chinese families and, on Sundays, domestic helpers. (p72)

Ocean Park An awesome theme park packed with locals and tourists during holidays. (p87)

OLESYA KUZNETSOVA/SHUTTERSTOCK ©

☑ Top Tips

▶ **The Leisure & Cultural Services Department website** (www.lcsd.gov.hk) lists the city's public parks and gardens.

▶ **Environmental Protection Department** (www.epd.gov.hk) lists of country and marine parks.

▶ For a longer list of Hong Kong's green green grass, visit **Lawnmap Hong Kong** (www.lawnmaphk.org), which also holds music events.

▶ All public parks have toilets and simple food stalls. Smoking is not allowed in parks.

Best
Shopping

Hong Kong has long been known as a place of neon-lit retail pilgrimage. This city is positively stuffed with swanky shopping malls and brand-name boutiques. All international brands worth their logo have outlets here. These are supplemented by the city's own retail trailblazers and a few creative local designers. Together they are Hong Kong's shrines and temples to style and consumption.

STEFAN IRVINE/GETTY IMAGES ©

Clothing

Shopping malls are the best places to find designer brands and luxury stores. Cool independents, opened by local designers and retailers, are more numerous in Sheung Wan, Wan Chai and Tsim Sha Tsui. The best hunting grounds for low-cost garments are the street markets.

Antiques

Hong Kong has a rich and colourful array of Asian (especially Chinese) antiques on offer, but serious buyers will restrict themselves to reputable antique shops and auction houses only. Forgeries and expert reproductions abound. Remember that most of the quality pieces are sold through auction houses such as Christie's, especially at its auctions in spring and autumn.

Digitals & Electronics

Hong Kong has a plethora of shops specialising in electronic and digital gadgets, but the product mix and prices may vary. Similarly, vendors' command of English can range from 'enough to close a deal' to 'reasonable'. Shopkeepers are generally honest but some have been known to sell display or second-hand items as new ones. All things considered, Wan Chai Computer Centre (p80) is your safest bet.

☑ Top Tips

▶ There's no sales tax in Hong Kong for most goods.

▶ Direct complaints to Hong Kong Tourism Board's **Quality Tourism Services** (QTS; ☎852 2508 1234; www.qtshk. com) or **Hong Kong Consumer Council** (☎852 29292222; www.consumer.org. hk; 9am-5.30pm Mon-Fri).

Stanley Market (p85)

Best for Fashion

Initial Hip urbanwear from multiple designers. (p109)

Kapok Hipster fashions from local and international designers. (p79)

Horizon Plaza Cut-rates on luxury goods and clothing in a 27-floor warehouse. (p93)

Best for Gifts

Temple Street Night Market Everything from chopsticks to jewellery – bargain hard. (p114)

Stanley Market Carved name chopsticks, satin baby shoes and more in a touristy but fun street market. (p85)

Picture This Cool vintage posters and antique books. (p41)

Lam Kie Yuen Tea Co Venerable tea shop with huge selection. (p39)

Livraria Portuguesa Stocks hard-to-find Macanese cookbooks. (p141)

Best for Food & Beverages

Shanghai Street Woks, mooncake moulds and other cooking implements galore. (p118)

Best for Books

Eslite Massive Taiwanese bookstore/cafe/gallery/toy store. (pictured top left; p79)

Kubrick Bookshop Café Excellent selection of highbrow fiction, art books and literary journals. (p121)

Livraria Portuguesa A good Portuguese and English bookstore in Macau. (p141)

Best
Markets

Best Specialty Markets

Cat Street Curios and (mostly) faux period pieces outdoors and in shops. (p34)

Jade Market Jade pendants, bracelets and other accessories in a covered setting. (p122)

Wholesale Fruit Market Century-old fruit market with an increasing number of stalls that open during the day. (p118)

Ap Lei Chau Market More varieties of live seafood than most other markets put together. (p90)

Best for Clothing

Stanley Market T-shirts, children's wear, Chinese-style garb in a maze of shops. (p85)

Ladies' Market This well-known market has dozens of stalls that sell cheap casual clothing. (p122)

Best for Fresh Food

Wan Chai's Markets (p79) Live produce, fresh noodles and all manner of spices along the street. (p79)

Ap Lei Chau Market Huge selection of live fish and crustaceans inside a government building. (p90)

Wholesale Fruit Market Retail is possible at this moody century-old market in Yau Ma Tei. (p118)

Best for Atmosphere

Temple Street Night Market Surrender to sounds, smells, sights and flavours unique to Hong Kong. (p114)

Wholesale Fruit Market These historic buildings are the most atmospheric in the wee hours. (p118)

Wan Chai's Markets (p79) The shops and stalls here are positively buzzing with life. (p79)

HOBBYMAN/500PX ©

Ap Lei Chau Market You'll see fishermen selling all kinds of live seafood. (p90)

Cat Street Where you can browse at leisure before heading to watering-holes of Soho (p34)

Most Eclectic

Temple Street Night Market Fortune tellers, Cantonese opera performers, hawkers, and street food. (pictured above; p114)

Stanley Market Clothes, Chinese souvenirs, lacework, even wet suits; and food nearby. (p85)

Wan Chai's Markets Food, funerary offerings, incense and spice shops along several streets. (p79)

Best
Activities

Best Beaches

South Bay A gem of a beach embraced by Hong Kong's French expatriate community. (p85)

Middle Bay Popular with scenesters, this quaint little beach lies between Repulse Bay and South Bay. (p85)

St Stephen's Beach A delightful bolt-hole close to Stanley main beach, but without the crowds. (p85)

Best for Pampering

Happy Foot Reflexology Centre Foot and body massage right in Lan Kwai Fong. (p51)

Flawless Hong Kong Feel-good massages and beauty treatments for glamour-conscious hipsters. (p50)

Best for Meeting People

Wan Kei Ho International Martial Arts Association Learn Shaolin Kung Fu with other expats and visitors. (p34)

Hong Kong Dolphin-watch Join travellers and animal-loving families to see the Chinese white dolphins. (p170)

Big Bus Company See Hong Kong from the roof of an open-topped double-decker. (p104)

Water Tours Take a leisurely cruise of Victoria Harbour on a junk-style boat. (p104)

Hong Kong House of Stories Join a tour of old Wan Chai. (p70)

Best Resources for Sports

South China Athletic Association (www.scaa.org.hk) Has sports facilities for hire.

Outdoor Sports (www.hkoutdoors.com)

Hong Kong Ultimate Frisbee Association (www.hkupa.com) Has twice-a-week pickups.

Casual Football Network (http://casualfootball.net) Has at least three games of football (soccer) a week.

KAY DULAY/GETTY IMAGES ©

☑ **Top Tips**

▸ **Hong Kong Tourism Board** (www.discoverhongkong.com) Has a full list of what's on.

▸ **Leisure and Cultural Services Department** (www.lcsd.gov.hk) Lists of fields, stadiums, beaches, swimming pools, water-sports centres etc, including equipment for hire.

Enjoy Hiking (http://hiking.gov.hk) Select trails by area, level of difficulty and duration.

Best
Fine Dining

Those with a large pocket are spoilt for choice in Hong Kong when it comes to haute cuisine, from braised abalone and lobster sashimi to the fancy molecular creations of the latest celebrity chef. Prices at the top addresses can be steep, but the city's gourmands don't seem to mind – the restaurants are fully booked almost every night.

LEE/LAKA.JONN.J/GETTY IMAGES ©

Haute Cantonese

Hong Kong's dominant cuisine is Cantonese, the most sophisticated of China's eight regional cuisines. The coastal location of Guangzhou (Canton), home of this style of cooking, provides access to some very costly marine life, such as deep-sea fish and gigantic lobsters. Even northern Chinese cooks acknowledge the superiority of their Cantonese colleagues in making the best of exclusive items such as dried abalone and sea cucumber.

Cantonese Cooking

Cantonese cooking is characterised by an obsession with freshness, complex methods, and the use of a wide range of ingredients. Flavours are delicate and balanced, achieved through the restrained use of seasoning and light-handed cooking techniques such as steaming and quick stir-frying.

Celebrity Chefs

Hong Kong's affluent and cosmopolitan population loves foreign food, especially Japanese and European. This is evidenced by the sheer number of exclusive sushi bars and European eateries you can find in town, and the number of eponymous restaurants opened by international celebrity chefs including Nobuyuki 'Nobu' Matsuhisa, Joël Robuchon and Pierre Gagnaire.

☑ **Top Tips**

A few of our favourite English-language food blogs for getting the up-to-date dirt on restaurants new and old:

▶ **That Food Cray** (www.thatfoodcray. com)

▶ **Sassy Hong Kong** (www.sassyhong-kong.com)

▶ **e-Ting** (www.e-tingfood. com)

▶ **Food Craver** (www.foodcraver.hk)

▶ **Hungry Hong Kong** (http://hun-gryhk.blogspot.hk)

Best Overall

Luk Yu Tea House
A meal at Hong Kong's most beautiful teahouse is to be savoured in every way. (p52)

Otto e Mezzo Bombana
Fine Italian dining at its best in Asia. (p37)

Boss Cantonese culinary wizardry in a tastefully understated environment. (p36)

Seventh Son Soups, steamed dishes, stir-fries, and dim sum, you name it, are all exceptional. (p73)

Serge et le Phoque
Chic modern French a truffle's throw from Wan Chai's wet markets. (p74)

Gaddi's The chandeliers are big but the service is warm, and the Gallic dishes top-notch. (p105)

Duddell's Sip champagne and enjoy art between mouthfuls of steaming dim sum. (p37)

Lung King Heen
Exquisite Michelin-crowned dim sum with a side of harbour views. (p37)

António Traditional Portuguese food refined in a quiet corner of Taipa Village in Macau. (p139)

Best for Chinese

Seventh Son
Masterful Cantonese cooking with service to match at a family-run establishment. (p73)

Boss Understated, but nonetheless a true boss when it comes to Cantonese fine dining. (p36)

Luk Yu Tea House
Cantonese classics done the old-fashioned way and served in vintage surrounds. (p52)

Best for European

Otto e Mezzo Bombana
Asia's only Italian restaurant with three Michelin stars lives up to its name. (p37)

Gaddi's The Peninsula's opulent French restaurant has been serving fine Gallic dishes since 1953. (p105)

Serge et le Phoque
Modern French in the heart of the Wan Chai market action. (p74)

Caprice Contemporary French in an opulent setting inside the Four Seasons. (p36)

Verandah Sunday brunch and proper afternoon tea under ceiling fans and other colonial trappings. (p85)

Best for Ambience

Luk Yu Tea House
Vintage Eastern art-deco decor with ceiling fans and stained-glass windows. (p52)

Duddell's Chic, design-oriented spaces enhanced by rotating artwork. (p37)

Serge et le Phoque
Watch butchers chop meat as you nibble in contemporary French luxury. (p74)

Yè Shanghai Dark, elegant interiors inspired by 1920s Shanghai. (p106)

Lung King Heen Sweeping views of Victoria Harbour from the Four Seasons Hotel. (p37)

Best for Upmarket Seafood

Hing Kee Restaurant
Choice seafood prepared the 'typhoon shelter' way in Tsim Sha Tsui. (p106)

Best
Budget Eats & Street Food

It is not difficult to eat well and cheaply in Hong Kong, compared to Tokyo or London. If you're looking to spend under HK$200 per person on a meal, there are good Chinese and South Asian options aplenty. For anything under HK$100, your dining room would be a noodle and congee shop, *cha chaan tang*, *dai pai dong* or fast-food chain.

AARON LIM/SHUTTERSTOCK ©

Cha Chaan Tang

The quintessential Hong Kong eatery, the tea cafe appeared in the 1940s to provide cheap Western-style snacks to people who couldn't afford Earl Grey and cucumber sandwiches. Most serve sandwiches, noodles, and tea or coffee with milk; some also serve rice dishes, curries and seafood, and Western-style pastries such as egg-custard tarts.

Dai Pai Dong

After WWII the government issued licences to the families of deceased civil servants so that they could operate food stalls for a living. The licence was physically big, so locals referred to these eateries as 'big licence stall' (*dai pai dong*). Traditionally, they are open-air hawker-style places, but many have been relocated to 'cooked-food centres' in buildings for easier management. Operators may serve anything from congee and sandwiches to hotpots and seafood.

☑ **Top Tips**

▶ To save money, go to a *cha chaan tang* (tea house) for the breakfast set or tea set. Portions are slightly smaller than a la carte. All sets come with a drink.

Best Dai Pai Dong

Temple Street Night Market Dine next to hawkers, Cantonese opera singers, and fortune-tellers. (p114)

Yue Hing Hong Kong–style milk tea and wacky sandwiches, consumed al fresco. (p53)

Tak Fat Beef Balls One stall inside Tsim Sha Tsui's last-remaining wet market. (p107)

Sei Yik Queues form for breakfast toast at

this half-hidden Stanley mainstay. (p90)

Ap Lei Chau Market Cooked Food Centre Cheap beer and seafood, (p90)

Best Cha Chaan Tang

Australia Dairy Company Long waits and surly service at this beloved Hong Kong institution. (p119)

Yue Hing Hong Kong–style sandwiches but with cabbage and peanut butter involved. (p53)

Lan Fong Yuen Known as the inventor of the Hong Kong–style 'pantyhose' milk tea. (p52)

Mido Café Atmosphere beats the food, especially by the upper-floor windows. (p120)

Best for Affordable Seafood

Aberdeen Fish Market Yee Hope Pre-ordering is required at this pearl tucked inside a fish market. (p89)

Ap Lei Chau Market Cooked Food Centre Freshly plucked sea life cooked at a noisy hawker centre. (p90)

BBQ Lobster You'll be overwhelmed by choice at

this grilled skewers place in Yau Ma Tei. (p120)

Hoi Kwong Seafood Restaurant Seafood and stir-fries in a crammed dining room. (p90)

Best Noodle & Congee Shops

Sun Sin Al dente strands in a delicious curry or tomato soup. (p119)

Nathan Congee and Noodle Fritters, rice dumpling, and fish skin salad. (p120)

Good Hope Noodle Michelin-crowned joint that's been around for half a century. (p120)

Mak's Noodle Silky wontons and egg noodles made the traditional way. (p52)

Kau Kee Beef brisket is served with noodles, tossed or in soup. (p51)

Tak Fat Beef Balls Beef balls laced with dried mandarin peel, served with noodles. (p107)

Best Chinese Budget Eateries

Ser Wong Fun Hearty old-school dishes, wine-infused liver sausage and snake soup. (p52)

Spring Deer This institution is synonymous with Peking duck. (p106)

Joy Hing Roasted Meat You'll need to queue for the luscious Michelin-lauded Cantonese barbeque. (p72)

Lock Cha Tea Shop Fine tea and veggie dim sum at the Museum of Tea Ware. (p74)

Din Tai Fung Shanghainese and northern classics by a worthy Taiwanese chain. (p106)

Best Budget Vegetarian

Gun Gei Healthy Vegetarian Delicious veggie meals above a wet market in Wan Chai. (p67)

Lock Cha Tea Shop Has a small but exquisite selection of vegetarian dim sum. (p74)

Yoga Interactive Vegetarian Multi-course Asian meals cooked by a yoga teacher. (p106)

Best Budget Non-Chinese Asian

Woodlands Nicely nuanced South Indian vegetarian dishes (p108)

Chicken HOF & Soju Korean The Korean fried chicken in five flavours. (p105)

Best
Dim Sum

KRUNJA/SHUTTERSTOCK ©

Best Overall

**City Hall
Maxim's Palace** Arguably the most famous of Hong Kong's dim sum palaces. (p35)

Seventh Son
An excellent spin-off of a restaurant known as 'tycoons' canteen'. (p73)

Luk Yu Tea House
This venerable teahouse was once an artist's haunt. (p52)

Lin Heung Tea House
Old-school cart dim sum in no-frills setting. (p38)

Best Budget Places

Yum Cha The morsels stare back at you as pig, bird, kitten and other edible cuties. (p105)

Lin Heung Tea House
The best breakfast after a night of drinking in Soho. (p38)

Tim Ho Wan, the Dim Sum Specialists
Sets the standard for high-quality budget dim sum in Asia. (p38)

Best Midrange Dim Sum

Luk Yu Tea House
Hong Kong's most famous teahouse does it the old-fashioned way. (p52)

Pure Veggie House
Vegetarian titbits that give their meaty cousins a run for their money. (p36)

Yè Shanghai Popular Cantonese selections plus delectable Shanghainese dumplings and pastries. (p106)

Best Luxury Titbits

Seventh Son The usual suspects beautifully done, and a few old-fashioned gems. (p73)

Lung King Heen
The Michelin-crowned creations sell out fast. (p37)

Boss Flavourful and healthy dim sum in a modern setting. (p36)

Duddell's Pair your titbits with champagne the way the regulars do. (p37)

Best
Culture

Thanks to its different trajectory of development from the rest of China, Hong Kong has a hybrid culture that is as complex as it is fascinating. Colonisation has westernised the city, yet the influences of traditional Lingnan culture, dominant in Guǎngdōng and other areas of southern China and brought here by the many artists, writers and musicians who fled China in the 1940s, are still very much apparent.

LONELY PLANET/GETTY IMAGES ©

Best for Local Culture

Hong Kong Museum of History All about Hong Kong: birth, teething, growing pains and all. (p99)

Middle Road Children's Playground Where local children of different ethnicities play together. (p102)

Wholesale Fruit Market A century-old fruit market that's alive and kicking. (p118)

Sino Centre A speciality mall for anime, discontinued magazines, figurines and other collectables. (p123)

G.O.D. Cheeky Hong Kong–inspired lifestyle items. (p57)

Sing-Along Parlours Fabulously shabby entertainment venues unique to Yau Ma Tei. (p115)

Mah-jong Parlours (p120) Where hardcore players gather for a game of mah-jong; no photos allowed. (p120)

Best for Indigenous Culture

Hong Kong Museum of History Learn about the customs and rituals of the Hakka, Puntay and Tanka. (p99)

Aberdeen Promenade Sights and smells of the 'people of the water' – Hong Kong's boat-dwelling community. (p87)

Pok Fu Lam Village Hong Kong Island's last surviving village and site of Hong Kong's first dairy (p89)

Best for Local Food Culture

Mido Café Atmospheric 1950s *cha chaan tang* (tea house), with retro tiles and all the works. (p120)

Luk Yu Tea House Vintage Eastern art-deco interiors and Lingnan-style paintings as impressive as the Canto dishes. (p52)

Australia Dairy Company Solid *cha chaan tang* staples served with surly efficiency. (p119)

Mammy Pancake The popular eggette and waffle sandwich with a twist. (p107)

Kung Lee Feeding the neighbourhood wholesome sugarcane juice since 1948. (p47)

Best
Drinking &
Nightlife

Energetic Hong Kong knows how to party and does so visibly and noisily. Drinking venues run the gamut from British-style pubs through hotel bars and hipster hang-outs, to karaoke bolt-holes aimed at a young Chinese clientele. The last few years have seen a heartening surge in the number of wine bars and live-music venues, catering to a diverse, discerning and fun-loving population.

MELISSA TSE/GETTY IMAGES ©

Happy Hour

During certain hours of the day, most pubs, bars and a few clubs give discounts on drinks (usually from a third to half off) or offer two-for-one deals. Happy hour is usually in the late afternoon or early evening – 4pm to 8pm, say – but times vary widely from place to place. Depending on the season, the day of the week and the location, some happy hours run from noon until 10pm, and some start up again after midnight.

Dress Code

Usually smart casual is good enough for most clubs, but patrons wearing shorts and flip-flops will not be admitted. Jeans are popular in Hong Kong and these are sometimes worn with heels or a blazer for a more put-together look. Hong Kong's clubbers can be style-conscious, so dress to impress!

☑ **Top Tips**

▶ Bars open at noon or 6pm and stay open until 2am to 6am; Wan Chai bars stay open the latest. Cafes usually open between 8am and 11am and close between 5pm and 11pm.

▶ For the latest information, check out **Time Out** (www. timeout.com.hk).

Club 71 (p47)

Best Overall

Tai Lung Fung Cocktails and old-fashioned flamboyance. (p75)

Club 71 Where all the activists, artists, musicians and the socially conscious go to rant and revel. (p47)

Best for a Cuppa

Peninsula Hong Kong The most elegant afternoon tea in the territory. (p100)

Cafe Corridor An intimate den with a lot of regulars. (p75)

Teakha Wake up and smell the jasmine at this elegant tea lounge. (p29)

Elephant Grounds Great brews including 'bulletproof coffee' and much-loved ice-cream sandwiches. (p76)

Lan Fong Yuen The classic spot to try Hong Kong's famous milk tea. (p52)

Best for Whisky

Butler It's either whisky or cocktails here, or whisky-based cocktails. (p108)

Angel's Share Whisky Bar It's all about the whisky here, especially the Irish variety. (p54)

Best for Wine

MyHouse Organic wines and vinyl in Causeway Bay. (p76)

Best for Cocktails

Butler Japanese cocktail and whisky bar in a quiet part of Tsim Sha Tsui. (p108)

Tai Lung Fung Charming retro setting awash in pink neon light. (p47)

Quinary Creative Asian-inspired cocktails in an elegant setting. (p55)

Best
Gay & Lesbian

While Hong Kong's gay scene may not have the vibrancy or visibility of cities like Sydney, it has made huge strides in recent years and now counts more than two dozen gay bars and clubs.

YE HANZHANG/SHUTTERSTOCK ©

Attitude to Homosexuality

It was only in 1991 that the *Crimes (Amendment) Ordinance* removed criminal penalties for homosexual acts between consenting adults over the age of 18 (criminal laws against male homosexuality were initially a product of British colonialism, with a maximum sentence of life imprisonment). Since then, gay groups have been lobbying for legislation to address the issue of discrimination on the grounds of sexual orientation, but to date there's still no law against it in Hong Kong. Neither is there legal recognition for same-sex marriages. That said, Hong Kong society is, in general, a lot more accepting of homosexuality than it was 10 years ago.

Best Bars & Clubs

Tivo Party with the drag hostesses on Sunday evenings at the Tivo Tea Dance. (p47)

T:ME An intimate gay bar in a back alley. (p55)

Boo This long-standing place in Kowloon is where 'bear' types like to hang. (p121)

Best for Shopping

Caroline Haven (p73) Trendy boutiques inside and around a 1960s Chinese residential block. (p73)

Hola Classic Affordable tailor-made clothing and shoes for men in Causeway Bay. (p78)

Numb Workshop Androgynous garments in black, white, grey and beige. (p80)

G.O.D. Lifestyle products with cheeky retro motifs. Horizon Plaza Furniture

☑ Top Tips

▶ **Dim Sum** (http://dimsum-hk.com) A free, monthly gay magazine with listings.

▶ **Les Peches** (p56) Hong Kong's premier lesbian organisation has monthly events for lesbians, bisexual women and their friends.

▶ **Utopia Asia** (www.utopia-asia.com/hkbars.htm) A website with listings of gay-friendly venues and events in town.

and off-season designer clothing. (p57)

Armoury For all things dapper, tailored and off the rack. (p41)

Best
Entertainment

VICTORN/SHUTTERSTOCK ©

Hong Kong has a lively cultural and entertainment calendar that sees the staging of music, drama and dance hailing from a plethora of traditions. The schedule of imported performances is nothing short of stellar. And every week, local arts companies and artists perform anything from Bach to stand-up to Cantonese opera and Chekhov.

Best for Art & Drama

Hong Kong Arts Centre Has theatres, art galleries and a cinema. (p78)

Fringe Club The Fringe Club hosts shows (art, drama, music) of an edgier nature. (p56)

Best for Indie Music

Focal Fair This indie hotspot has hosted local and international shows from hardcore punk to noise. (p77)

Fringe Club Concerts inside the historic Fringe Dairy. (p56)

Street Music Concert Series Under-the-stars concerts with eclectic line-ups (p77)

Best for Jazz & Rock

Peel Fresco Live jazz in Soho almost every day of the week. (p56)

Fringe Club Jazz figures prominently on the Fringe Club's busy entertainment calendar. (p56)

Best Festivals for Entertainment

Hong Kong Arts Festival Featuring some of the world's most revered performers. (p78)

Clockenflap This outdoor indie music event is the highlight of the city's live-music calendar. (p78)

Hong Kong International Film Festival Asia's top film festival takes place on the Central waterfront. (p78)

☑ Top Tips

▶ To see what's on, check out **Artmap** (www.artmap.com. hk), **Artslink** (www. hkac.org.hk) and **Time Out** (www. timeout.com.hk)

▶ For tickets & booking, see **Urbtix** (www. urbtix.hk). **HK Ticketing** (www.hkticketing. com) have tickets to every major event in Hong Kong. You can book through them or purchase tickets at the performance venues.

Hong Kong Jazz Festival When local jazz lovers' get to see the greats live. (☉ Sep, Oct or Nov)

Best
For Kids

Hong Kong is a great destination for kids, though the crowds, traffic and pollution might take a little getting used to. Food and sanitation are of a high standard. The city is jam-packed with things to entertain the young ones.

Dolphin-watching

Hong Kong Dolphinwatch (香港海豚觀察; ☎852 2984 1414; www.hkdolphinwatch.com; 15th fl, Middle Block, 1528A Star House, 3 Salisbury Rd, Tsim Sha Tsui; adult/child HK$420/210; ⏱cruises Wed, Fri & Sun) was founded in 1995 to raise awareness of Hong Kong's wonderful pink dolphins and promote responsible ecotourism. It offers 2½-hour cruises to see them in their natural habitat. About 97% of the cruises result in the sighting of at least one dolphin; if none are spotted, passengers are offered a free trip.

Guides assemble in the lobby of the **Kowloon Hotel Hong Kong** (九龍酒店; www.thekowloonhotel. com; 19-21 Nathan Rd, Tsim Sha Tsui; Ⓜ Tsim Sha Tsui, exit E) in Tsim Sha Tsui at 9am for the bus to Tung Chung via the Tsing Ma Bridge, from where the boat departs; the tours return at 1pm.

Between 100 and 200 misnamed Chinese white dolphins (*Sousa chinensis*) – they are actually bubble-gum pink – inhabit the coastal waters around Hong Kong, finding the brackish waters of the Pearl River estuary to be the perfect habitat. Unfortunately these glorious mammals, which are also called Indo-Pacific humpback dolphins, are being threatened by environmental pollution, and their numbers are dwindling.

LEUNG CHOPAN/GETTY IMAGES ©

Best Child-Friendly Museums

Hong Kong Science Museum Three storeys of action-packed displays are a huge attraction for toddlers to teens. (p103)

Hong Kong Museum of History Brings the city's history to life in colourful ways. (p99)

Hong Kong Maritime Museum Pirate mannequins, real shipwreck treasures, and a metal diving suit. (p32)

Hong Kong Space Museum Toddlers can test their motor skills; older kids will enjoy the Omnimax films. (p103)

Comix Home Base Displays, a library and video footage on Hong Kong's comic-book history. (p71)

Best Parks for Children

Ocean Park Hong Kong's premier amusement park offers mechanical rides, a top aquarium, pandas and cable-cars. (p87)

Hong Kong Park Ponds with ducks, swans and turtles, and a massive forest-like aviary. (p64)

Middle Road Children's Playground Swings, slides, and fancy climbing facilities for children of all ages. (p102)

Kowloon Park Plenty of running room, lakes with waterfowl, playgrounds, swimming pools and an aviary. (p100)

Victoria Peak Garden Dappled lawns, sundials and faux-Victoria pillars make this ideal for a family picnic. (p42)

Best Rides

Peak Tram Children may be fascinated by the ride on the gravity-defying Peak Tram. (pictured; p42)

Star Ferry Cruise Liner, barge, hydrofoil...Your mini-mariner will have a blast naming passing vessels. (p176)

Trams Watching the world from a vehicle that rattles, clanks and sways can be exhilarating. (p176)

Best Shopping

Tai Yuen St 'Toy street' is lined with traditional toy shops catering to youngsters. (p79)

Stanley Market Reasonably-priced clothes, shoes and hair accessories. (p85)

Horizon Plaza A multi-storey factory building with megastores selling kids' books and clothing. (p93)

PMQ Cute, cartoon-themed lifestyle stores and a vintage toy shop, with breezy corridors to run around in. (p50)

Best Dining for Kids

Mammy Pancake Hong Kong–style eggettes and waffle sandwiches in creative flavours. (p107)

Tai Cheong Bakery Egg-custard tarts, airy beignets, and other lovely local pastries. (p53)

Kung Lee Fresh sugar-cane juice is a cure for infections and the common cold. (p47)

Chicken HOF & Soju Korean Fried chicken! But be sure not to get the spicy versions. (p105)

Yue Hing Imagine a spam and egg sandwich with peanut butter! (p53)

Jumbo Kingdom Floating Restaurant A popular movie set decked out in dragon-and-phoenix carvings. (p88)

Dumpling Yuan Nine delicious varieties of dumplings will keep junior fed and your wallet happy. (p51)

♥ Best
For Free

Best Art for Free

Museum of Art
A treasure trove of Hong Kong and Chinese art; it's free on Wednesdays. (p97)

Museum of Tea Ware
An elegant showcase of vintage tea ware inside Hong Kong Park. (p65)

Blindspot Gallery
Specialising in showing the works of Hong Kong and Asian photographers. (p89)

Best Music for Free

Street Music Concert Series
(p77) Excellent twice monthly line-ups from classical through jazz to indie. (p77)

Senses 99
Free jamming every weekend in an upstairs music dive in Sheung Wan. (p56)

Best Cheap & Cheerful

Tram
For HK$2.30 you can rattle your way through the urban canyon of high-rises on a tram. (p176)

Star Ferry
Give up pocket change for the voyage of a lifetime on the Star Ferry. (p176)

Horse-racing
For only HK$10, you can experience a night at the races. (p62)

Thrill Rides
White-knuckle bus rides on routes 314, 14, 6, H1 and H2.

LONELY PLANET/GETTY IMAGES ©

☑ Top Tips

▶ For a cheaper trip to the movies, visit on Tuesdays, when you can pay HK$10 to HK$30 less for a ticket.

Survival Guide

Survival Guide

Before You Go

When to Go

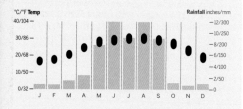

°C/°F Temp
Rainfall inches/mm

→ Spring (Mar-May)
Asia's top film festival, a rugby tournament, an art fair and deities' birthdays await in the warm and wet city.

→ Summer (Jun-Aug)
Something hot (the beach, a new wardrobe), something wet (dragon-boat races, beer): your antidotes to sultry summers.

→ Autumn (Sep-Nov)
Head for the hills by day, enjoy an outdoor concert by night – autumn is the best time to visit Hong Kong.

→ Winter (Dec-Feb)
Chilly with occasional rain, Hong Kong celebrates Chinese New Year under Christmas lights.

Book Your Stay

Hong Kong offers a full range of accommodation, from closet-sized rooms to palatial suites. Most hotels on Hong Kong Island are between Central and Causeway Bay; in Kowloon, they fall around Nathan Rd, where you'll also find budget places. During low season prices fall sharply, particularly the midrange and top-end options, when booking online can get you discounts of up to 60%.

Useful Websites

→ Lonely Planet
(lonelyplanet.com/china/hong-kong/hotels) Book LP's top accommodation picks online.

→ Hotel.com
(www.hotels.com/Hong-Kong) Specialises in cheap lodging.

→ Discover Hong Kong
(www.discoverhongkong.com) Provides a hotel search based on location and facilities.

Asia Travel (www. hongkonghotels.com) Offers competitive deals.

Best Budget

Campus Hong Kong (www.campushk.com) Live like royalty in a student hostel (if you manage to book a room, that is) in Tsuen Wan.

YHA Mei Ho House Youth Hostel (www. meihohouse.hk) Fine views and immaculate rooms in an off-the-way historic housing estate.

Best Midrange

Twenty One Whitfield Clean, bright rooms available for daily and monthly stays in Tin Hau.

Tuve Sleek, (www.tuve.hk) industrial chic rooms, an artsy reception area, and helpful staff in Tin Hau.

Best Top End

Peninsula Hong Kong (www.peninsula.com) One of the most elegant and richly storied hotels in Asia.

Hotel Indigo Chinese-inspired design, state-of-the-art facilities and exceptional service make this a winner.

Arriving in Hong Kong

....

Hong Kong International Airport

➡ Airport Express MTR train to city centre from 5.54am to 12.48am, HK$90 to HK$100; buses to various parts of Hong Kong from 6am to 12.30am, HK$19 to HK$48; taxi to city centre HK$220 to HK$360.

➡ Lo Wu and Lok Ma Chau MTR train to city centre from 5.55am to 12.30am (Lo Wu), from 6.38am to 10.55pm (Lok Ma Chau), HK$37 to HK$48.

Hong Kong-Macau Ferry Terminal

➡ MTR train (Sheung Wan) to city centre from the terminal (see Map p30, D1) from 6.05am to 12.46am, HK$4.50 to HK$13; taxi HK$20 to HK$100.

China Ferry Terminal

➡ MTR train (Tsim Sha Tsui) from the terminal (see Map p98, A2) to city centre from 6.11am to 12.54am, HK$4.50 to HK$12; taxi HK$20 to HK$100.

Tickets & Passes

A prepaid Octopus Card can be used on most forms of public transport. They can be bought at any MTR station, and topped up at MTR stations and convenience stores.

If visiting for over two days, buy an Octopus Card; it will save you up to 5% per trip and you won't have to buy tickets and pay exact fares on buses.

For shorter stays, buy a one-day or three-day pass for unlimited rides on the MTR. Available at any MTR station.

Getting Around

Bus

Hong Kong's extensive bus system will take you just about anywhere in the territory.

Departures Most buses run from 5.30am or 6am until midnight or 12.30am, though there are smaller numbers of night buses that run from 12.45am to 5am or later.

Fares Bus fares cost HK$4 to HK$46, depending on the destination. Fares for night buses cost from HK$7 to HK$32. You will need exact change or an Octopus card.

Route information Figuring out which bus you want can be difficult, but **City Bus** and **New World First Bus**, owned by the same company (www.nwstbus.com.hk), plus **Kowloon Motor Bus** (www.kmb.hk) provide a user-friendly route search on their websites. KMB also has a route app for smartphones.

Taxi

Hong Kong taxis are a bargain compared to taxis in other world-class cities. Taxi fares from the Airport:

DESTINATION	FARE (HK$)
Central, Admiralty, Wan Chai, Causeway Bay (Hong Kong Island)	280-320
Tsim Sha Tsui, Jordan, Yau Ma Tei, Mong Kok, Hung Hom (Kowloon)	230-250
Sha Tin (New Territories)	280
Tsuen Wan (New Territories)	200
Tung Chung (Lantau)	45-55

In addition to the fares listed, passengers have to pay HK$5 for every piece of baggage that is carried inside the baggage compartment.

Ferry

The **Star Ferry** (天星小輪; Map p30; ☏ 852 2367 7065; www.starferry.com.hk; adult HK$2.50-3.40, child HK$1.50-2.10; ⏱ every 6-12min, 6.30am-11.30pm; Ⓜ Hong Kong, exit A2) connects Hong Kong Island and Kowloon Peninsula via Victoria Harbour (see Map p98, B4); it runs from 6.30am-11.30pm; fares are HK$2.50 to HK$3.40. Modern ferry fleets run between Central and the outlying islands.

Metro

The **Mass Transit Railway** (MTR; ☏ 852 2881 8888; www.mtr.com.hk; fares HK$4-25) is the quickest way to get to most destinations in Hong Kong, though it costs slightly more than bus travel.

Tram

For a flat fare of HK$2.30 (dropped in a box beside the driver as you disembark) you can rattle along the northern coast of Hong Kong Island on a double-decker **tram** (☏ 852 2548 7102; www.hktramways.com; fares HK$2.30; ⏱ 6am-midnight) for as far as you like, over 16km of track.

Essential Information

Business Hours

The following list summarises standard opening hours.

Banks 9am to 4.30pm or 5.30pm Monday to Friday, 9am to 12.30pm Saturday.

Museums 10am to between 5pm and 9pm; closed Monday, Tuesday or Thursday.

Offices 9am to 5.30pm or 6pm Monday to Friday (lunch hour 1pm to 2pm).

Restaurants 11am to 3pm and 6pm to 11pm.

Shops Usually 10am to 8pm.

Customs Regulations

➡ The duty-free allowance for visitors arriving in Hong Kong (including those coming from Macau and mainland China) is 19 cigarettes (or one cigar or 25g of tobacco) and 1L of spirits.

Electricity

220V/50Hz

Emergency

➡ Fire, Police & Ambulance (999)

Internet Access

➡ **Free wi-fi** Available in hotels and public areas, including the airport, public libraries, key cultural and recreational centres, large parks, major MTR stations, shopping malls and almost all urban cafes and bars. You can also get a free 60-minute PCCW Wi-Fi pass, available at HKTB visitor centres.

➡ **PCCW account** You can purchase a PCCW account online or at convenience stores and PCCW stores, and access the internet via any of PCCW's 7000-plus wi-fi hot spots in Hong Kong.

Money

ATMs

➡ Most ATMs are linked up to international money systems such as Cirrus, Maestro, Plus and Visa Electron.

➡ Some of HSBC's so-called Electronic Money machines offer cash withdrawal facilities for Visa and MasterCard holders.

➡ American Express (Amex) cardholders have access to Jetco ATMs and can withdraw local currency and travellers cheques at Express Cash ATMs in town.

Credit Cards

➡ The most widely accepted cards are Visa, MasterCard, Amex, Diners Club and JCB – pretty much in that order.

➡ Some shops add a surcharge to offset the commission charged by credit companies, which can range from 2.5% to 7%.

→ If a card is lost or stolen, you must inform both the police and the issuing company as soon as possible; otherwise you may have to pay for the purchases that have been racked up on your card.

Local Currency

→ Hong Kong uses Hong Kong currency but some shops and restaurants also accept rénmínbì.

→ Macau uses pataca and most places accept Hong Kong currency as well.

Tipping

→ **Hotels** A HK$10 or HK$20 note for the porter; gratuity for cleaning staff at your discretion.

→ **Restaurants** Most eateries, except very cheap places, impose a 10% to 15% service charge, but it is normal to still tip a little (under 5%) if you're happy with the experience. At budget joints, just rounding it off to the nearest HK$10 is fine.

→ **Pubs and cafes** Not expected unless table service is provided, then something under 5% of your bill.

Left Luggage

MTR train and ferry

Left-luggage lockers/services are in major stations, including Hung Hom station, Kowloon station and Hong Kong station; the West Tower of **Shun Tak Centre**

(信德中心; 200 Connaught Rd Central, Hong Kong) in Sheung Wan (see Map p30, D1) from where the Macau ferry departs; and the China ferry terminal in Tsim Sha Tsui. Lockers cost between HK$20 and HK$30 per hour (depending on size).

Airport The Hong Kong International Airport provides a left-luggage service.

Accommodation Most hotels and even some guesthouses and hostels have left-luggage rooms and will let you leave your gear behind, even if you've already checked out and won't be staying on your return. There is usually a charge for this

Dos & Don'ts

Greetings Just wave and say 'Hi' and 'Bye' when meeting for the first time and when saying goodbye.

Dining At budget places, people think nothing of sticking their chopsticks into a communal dish. Better restaurants provide separate serving spoons with each dish; if they're provided, use them. Don't be afraid to ask for a fork if you can't manage chopsticks.

Queues Hong Kongers line up for everything. Attempts to 'jump the queue' are frowned upon.

Bargaining Haggling over the price of goods is not expected in shops. Do bargain when buying from street vendors (but not in food markets).

ervice, so be sure to enquire first.

Public Holidays

Western and Chinese culture combine to create an interesting mix – and number – of public holidays in Hong Kong. Determining the exact date of some of them is tricky, as there are traditionally two calendars in use: the Gregorian solar (or Western) calendar and the Chinese lunar calendar.

New Year's Day
1 January

Chinese New Year
16 February 2018, 5 February 2019

Easter
14–17 April 2017, 30 March–2 April 2018

Ching Ming
5 April 2017, 5 April 2018

Labour Day 1 May

Buddha's Birthday
3 May 2017, 22 May 2018

Dragon Boat (Tuen Ng) Festival
30 May 2017, 18 June 2018

Hong Kong SAR Establishment Day
1 July

Mid-Autumn Festival
4 October 2017, 24 September 2018

China National Day
1 October

Chung Yeung
28 October 2017, 17 October 2018

Christmas Day
25 December

Boxing Day
26 December

Tourist Information

➡ **China Travel Service** Has four counters at the airport.

➡ **Hong Kong Tourism Board** (www.discoverhk. com) Has helpful and welcoming staff, and reams of information – most of it free. Also sells a few useful publications.

➡ **iCyberlink** Outside these centres, and at several other places in the territory, you'll be

Telephone

Access Any GSM-compatible phone can be used here.

Coverage Mobile phones work everywhere, including in the harbour tunnels and on the MTR.

Purchase Service providers have mobile phones and accessories along with rechargeable SIM cards for sale from HK$98. Local calls cost between 6¢ and 12¢ a minute (calls to the mainland are about HK$1.80/minute).

Both the telephone directory and the *Yellow Pages* can be consulted online at www.yp.com.hk.

USEFUL TELEPHONE NUMBERS

International dialling code	☎ 001
International directory enquiries	☎ 10015
Local directory enquiries	☎ 1081
Reverse-charge/collect calls	☎ 10010
Time and temperature	☎ 18501
Weather	☎ 187 8200

able to find iCyberlink screens, from which you can access the HKTB website and database 24 hours a day.

➡ **Visitor centres** In addition to the office at the Star Ferry Visitor Concourse, HKTB has visitor centres at the airport, The Peak, and at the border to mainland China.

Tours

➡ There are tours available to just about anywhere in the territory and they can make a good option if you have limited time, want more in-depth knowledge in a short time, or don't want to deal with public transport.

➡ Some tours are standard excursions covering major sights, while others may give you a deeper experience of a neighbourhood. There are also speciality tours such as food tours, WWII tours and architecture tours.

➡ **Hong Kong Tourism Board** (www.discoverhk. com) has recommendations, and tours run by individual companies can usually be booked at any HKTB branch.

Travellers with Disabilities

➡ People with mobility issues have to cope with substantial obstacles in Hong Kong, including the stairs at many MTR stations, as well as pedestrian overpasses, narrow

and crowded footpaths, and steep hills.

➡ Some buses are accessible by wheelchair, taxis are never hard to find, most buildings have lifts (many with Braille panels) and MTR stations have Braille maps with recorded information. Wheelchairs can negotiate the lower decks of most ferries.

➡ **Easy Travel Access** (www.rehabsociety.org. hk) offers tours and accessible transport services.

➡ **Transport Department** (www.td.gov. hk) provides guides to public transportation, parking and pedestrian crossing for people with disabilities.

Language

Cantonese is the most popular Chinese dialect in Hong Kong. Cantonese speakers can read Chinese characters, but will pronounce many characters differently from a Mandarin speaker.

Cantonese has 'tonal' quality – the raising and lowering of pitch on certain syllables. Tones fall on vowels and on the consonant **n**. Our pronunciation guides show five tones, indicated by accent marks – **à** (high), **á** (high rising), **à** (low falling), **á** (low rising), **a** (low) – plus a level tone (**a**).

To enhance your trip with a phrasebook, visit **lonelyplanet.com**.

Basics

Hello.	哈佬。	hàa·ló
Goodbye.	再見。	joy·gin
How are you?	你幾好啊嗎？	láy gáy hó à maa
Fine.	幾好。	gáy hó
Please ...	唔該……	ǹg·gòy ...
Thank you.	多謝。	dàw·je
Excuse me.	對唔住。	deui·ǹg·jew
Sorry.	對唔住。	deui·ǹg·jew
Yes.	係。	hai
No.	不係。	ǹg·hai

Do you speak English?
你識唔識講英文啊 | láy sìk·ǹg·sìk gáwng yìng·mán aa

I don't understand.
我唔明。 | ngáw ǹg mìng

Eating & Drinking

I'd like..., please.
唔該我要…… | ǹg·gòy ngáw yiu ...

a table for two	兩位嘅檯	léung wái ge tóy
the drink list	酒料單	jáu·liú·dàan
the menu	菜單	choy·dàan
beer	啤酒	bè·jáu
coffee	咖啡	gaa·fè

I don't eat ...
我唔吃…… | ngáw ǹg sik ...

fish	魚	yéw
poultry	雞鴨鵝	gài ngaap ngàw
red meat	牛羊肉	ngàu yèung yuk

Cheers!
乾杯！ | gàwn·buì

That was delicious.
真好味。 | jàn hó·may

I'd like the bill, please.
唔該我要埋單。 | ǹg·gòy ngáw yiu màai·dàan

Shopping

I'd like to buy ...
我想買…… | ngáw séung máai ...

I'm just looking.
睇下。 | tái haa

How much is it?
幾多錢? | gáy·dàw chín

That's too expensive.

太貴啦。 taai gwai laa

Can you lower the price?

可唔可以平 háw·ǹg·háw·yí pèng
啲呀？ dì aa

Emergencies

Help!
救命！ gau·meng

Go away!
走開！ jáu·hòy

Call a doctor!
快啲叫醫生! faai·dì giu yì·sàng

Call the police!
快啲叫警察! faai·dì giu gíng·chaat

I'm lost.
我蕩失路。 ngáw dawng·sàk·lo

I'm sick.
我病咗。 ngáw beng·jáw

Where are the toilets?
廁所喺邊度？ chi·sáw hái bìn·do

Time & Numbers

What time is it?
而家 yi·gàa
幾點鐘？ gáy·dím·jùng

It's (10) o'clock.
(十)點鐘。 (sap)·dím·jùng

Half past (10).
(十)點半。 (sap)·dím bun

morning	朝早	jiù·jó
afternoon	下晝	haa·jau
evening	夜晚	ye·máan
yesterday	寢日	kàm·yat
today	今日	gàm·yat
tomorrow	听日	tìng·yat

1	一	yàt
2	二	yi
3	三	sàam
4	四	say
5	五	ńg
6	六	luk
7	七	chàt
8	八	baat
9	九	gáu
10	十	sap

Transport & Directions

Where's ...?
……喺邊度？ ... hái bìn·do

What's the address?
地址係？ day·jí hai

How do I get there?
點樣去？ dím·yéung heui

How far is it?
有幾遠？ yáu gáy yéwn

Can you show me (on the map)?
你可唔可以 láy háw·ǹg·háw·yí
(喺地圖度)指俾 (hái day·to do) jí báy
我睇我喺邊度？ ngáw tái ngáw hái bìn·do

When's the next bus?
下一班巴士 haa·yàt·bàan bàa·sí
幾點開？ gáy dím hòy

A ticket to ...
一張去…… yàt jèung heui ...
嘅飛。 ge fày

Does it stop at ...?
會唔會喺 wuí·ǹg·wuí hái
……停呀？ ... tìng aa

I'd like to get off at ...
我要喺…… ngáw yiu hái ...
落車。 lawk·chè

Behind the Scenes

Send Us Your Feedback

We love to hear from travellers – your comments help make our books better. We read every word, and we guarantee that your feedback goes straight to the authors. Visit **lonelyplanet.com/contact** to submit your updates and suggestions.

Note: We may edit, reproduce and incorporate your comments in Lonely Planet products such as guidebooks, websites and digital products, so let us know if you don't want your comments reproduced or your name acknowledged. For a copy of our privacy policy visit lonelyplanet.com/privacy.

Piera's Thanks

Much gratitude to Alvin, CSY and Janine for their generous assistance. Thanks also to my co-author on the Hong Kong City Guide Emily Matchar for her contribution. Finally, I must acknowledge my husband, Kontau, and my daughter, Clio, for their loving support.

Acknowledgements

Cover photograph: Shop selling Chinese New Year decorations; Ian Trower/AWL©

This Book

This 6th edition of Lonely Planet's *Pocket Hong Kong* guidebook was researched and written by Piera Chen and Emily Matchar. The previous two editions were also written by Piera Chen. This guidebook was produced by the following:

Destination Editor
Megan Eaves

Product Editors
Jessica Ryan, Sasha Drew

Senior Cartographer
Julie Sheridan

Book Designer
Gwen Cotter

Assisting Editors
Judith Bamber, Lauren O'Connell, Simon Williamson

Cover Researcher
Naomi Parker

Thanks to

Cheree Broughton, Jennifer Carey, Neill Coen, Daniel Corbett Alastair Cox, Andreas Höcherl, Andi Jones, Lauren Keith, Sandie Kestell, Kate Kiely, Indra Kilfoyle, Alison Lyall, Dan Moore, Catherine Naghten, Claire Naylor, Karyn Noble, Karen Ransome, Ellie Simpson, Angela Tinson,

Index

See also separate subindexes for:

✪ **Eating p187**

✪ **Drinking p187**

✪ **Entertainment p188**

✪ **Shopping p188**

Sights 000
Map Pages **000**